It's Never Too Late to Love a Computer

It's Never Too Late to Love a Computer

a friendly first guide *by Abby Stokes*

Illustrations **by Jeff Seaver**

WORKMAN PUBLISHING • NEW YORK

Library of Congress Cataloging-in-Publication Data
Stokes, Abby.
It's never too late to love a computer/by Abby Stokes
p. cm.
ISBN 0-7611-1481-5 (alk. paper)
1. Microcomputers. I. Title

QA76.5 S7824 2000
004.16—dc21   99-047845

Author photo © 2000 by Laura Straus, NY
Depictions of computer screens by Shi Chen and Abby Stokes

Workman books are available at special discounts when purchased in bulk for
premiums and sales promotions as well as for fund-raising or educational use.
Special editions or book excerpts can also be created to specification. For details,
contact the Special Sales Director at the address below.

Workman Publishing Company, Inc.
708 Broadway
New York, NY 10003-9555
www.workman.com

Manufactured in the United States of America

First Printing February 2001
10 9 8 7 6 5 4 3 2 1

For Nana

*I dedicate this book
to my 95-year-old grandmother,
Evelyn Angell Pemberton,
who still has plenty of time
to love the computer.*

Thank You, Thank You, Thank You

I thank my lucky stars every day for the incredible group of family and friends that I am privileged to call my loved ones. My lucky stars also have me living in the most exciting city in the world, where I spend my time doing things I truly enjoy. If that isn't enough to be grateful for, this book project dropped into my lap two years ago. In that regard I would like to specifically thank the following people: Mom, Eve, and Sherri, who willingly and supportively listened to *every* draft; Dan Tucker and Megan McFarland, whose professional experience and advice skillfully guided me through this process; Letitia Ord, without whose editing skills I might have constructed more sentences like this one; Laura Straus, for her matchmaking talents; Roger Straus, Lisa MacDonald, and High Tide for their unwarranted confidence in me; Joe Capuana, who fifteen years ago gently held my hand through my first computer experience; Ellen Morgenstern, Judy Hirsh, Paul Gamarello, David Schiller, Sally Kovalchick, Margot Herrera, Morris Taub, Jeff Seaver, Monica McCready and the entire team at Workman; Henry Hirsch, who has made *great* progress on the computer despite my distracting him with publishing questions along the way; all my other students, who thought they were learning from me, when the reverse was usually the case; and, above all, you for buying this book and loving it so much that you buy it for all your friends.

Contents

Go for a Test-Drive

Let the Shopping Begin

Baby's First Day Home

The Newlywed Game

Appendices

A Word Before You Begin

When I was in second grade, I proudly went to the library to sign out my first book with chapters. After finishing the book, I confessed to my sister, Eve, that I found it a bit confusing. She pointed out what was supposed to be obvious, but obviously wasn't to me—the chapters were meant to be read in sequence. Who knew?

Read this book in sequence at your own pace, and it will unveil the basics that you need to know about the computer in order to make a sound computer purchase, set it up in your home and get connected to the Internet. This book is intended to demystify the computer, not to explain the gory inner workings of the machine. Every day we use devices such as a car, the telephone or the TV but have no idea how they really work. Nonetheless, we do work them. The computer is no different.

You will notice that certain reminders, instructions and warnings are repeated throughout the book. This is so you can follow along with the text without having to fish around for help in earlier chapters. Be forewarned that once you arrive at Chapter 10, it is all hands-on instruction and will definitely be overwhelming if you try to visualize what is being discussed. If you haven't bought your computer by then, make sure that you're sitting in front of someone else's before you continue.

Take a deep breath and begin your journey. You're going to be pleasantly surprised at how much easier it is than you anticipated. Take breaks from the book whenever you want, and reread things that are unclear. Before you know it, you'll be skillfully "surfing the net" and e-mailing all your friends!

Abby

P.S. To protect the innocent, the names have been changed throughout the book.

There Is Nothing to Fear but Technology Itself

1 Bring the World to Your Fingertips

Research, find and buy anything you can imagine, and communicate with loved ones . . . without leaving home

My mother still can't program her VCR. Even better, for the first week after she buys a new car, she'll only drive it in the Stop & Shop parking lot. Once she feels comfortable enough to take it on the road, it's still a few months before the windshield wipers stop being activated whenever she means to signal a right turn. All that said, I am incredibly proud of her for joining the community of the computer savvy. Mom had never shown any interest in computers, but like so many seniors, she knew she was missing out on something when she began to notice that every article she read ended with "Visit us on the Internet at *www.[insert almost anything here].com.*"

"Peach, what is the Internet?"

"Think of the computer as a combination television set and typewriter. Then think of the Internet as a library. You can find information on absolutely anything you can dream up on the Internet by accessing different web sites—as you would books in a library. Just type in what you want to learn about, and it will appear in front of you in the form of pictures, text and sound."

A web site is like a book. Instead of going to the library and looking up a title in the card catalog, you go to the computer and type in a web site address.

Because there can be more than one web site for a given subject, you'll have many choices available to you. Each web site is designed individually, just as books are written individually by different authors.

Anyone can have a web site—even you. All that is needed is the desire to convey information and the willingness to pay a small annual fee to a company to register the name of your web site.

A few months after my mother first asked me about the Internet, she visited me in New York and wanted to see a Broadway musical. This was the perfect opportunity to show her what a computer can do, what the Internet has to offer and how I make my living. I turned on my computer, opened my service provider's software, typed in my password to get on the Internet and then typed in *www.theatre.com* (the web site address for an agency that sells theater tickets), and like magic, their web site appeared on the screen of my computer. I picked the show we wanted to see and the date that was best for us. Next, the seating chart appeared on the screen and we chose our seats. Then I ordered the tickets and typed in the address to which they should be mailed.

Mom was impressed. I've been teaching people how to maneuver around the Internet for a few years now, and it continues to amaze me with the infinite ways that it can benefit those who use it. The Internet allows you to track investments, research family genealogy, contact buddies, purchase a new car, auction a coin collection, search for the best deal on airline tickets and so much more.

Convincing Mom Continues . . .

The ease with which we were able to purchase the theater tickets via the computer had my mother intrigued.

"What else can the Internet do?"

"I can't tell you everything it can do, Mom, because it's constantly evolving. I don't think anyone really knows its full capabilities. But I'll give you some examples of what I think is fun and practical about it."

Mom had lost track of a dear friend of hers several years ago and, after much effort, sadly gave up on finding her. I signed on to the Internet and typed in *www.switchboard.com* (a web site where you can search for people and businesses). A form appeared on the screen of my computer, on which I typed her friend's name and some additional information. Within a few seconds there were seven listings of people with the same name as Mom's long-lost friend. The listings that appeared included telephone numbers, street addresses and e-mail addresses. The happy ending is that Mom found her friend. From that moment on she was hooked on the computer.

Shirley, one of my mother's friends, suffers from a very rare cancer. After she became hooked on the computer, not only did she find detailed information about her specific form of cancer and alternative treatment ideas, but she also found a group of people with the same condition. She now communicates with some of them on a daily basis. All of this is done through her computer, which enables her to be involved in the world around her even when she is housebound.

To say that the Internet can give you information on *anything* you can dream up may sound like a huge overstatement, but it's true.

"*I had no idea what the computer could do for me, but I knew that if I didn't try it soon, I never would. Now I use it for everything. . . . I write the newsletter and maintain the mailing list for my church. I love finding out all kinds of information on the Internet and I'm a big fan of e-mail.***"**

—Marsha

A Taste of What Some People Do with the Internet

Sophie always has an interesting list of things she wants to find out about on the Internet. During one of our lessons we visited web sites that gave information about renting a house on Martha's Vineyard, tracked down an artist whose work she wanted to buy and found a doormat with Jack Russell terriers emblazoned on it.

By typing "Martha's Vineyard rentals" in a search engine (which I'll explain to you later), we came upon more than a dozen web sites, many of them with photos of the interiors and exteriors of the houses available. While looking at a photo of one of the rentals, we noticed the words "how to get here" on the screen. We clicked on the words and a different web site appeared that offered us driving directions and a map that showed the best route. Sophie printed the directions and set them aside to put in her car's glove compartment.

Then came the mission of tracking down the artist whose work she liked. First we typed in the artist's name, but that didn't work. Then she remembered what gallery showed his work and typed that in. Not only did it give us contact information, but one of his paintings was featured on the web site as well.

On to the doormat. That took a little ingenuity. We searched for "doormats" and "doormats with dogs." We found tons of doormats and a surprising number of doormats with dogs, but not the right kind of dog. Then we searched for "Jack Russell terriers." We found a great-looking doormat and bought it over the Internet with her credit card. It was delivered the next week. We both had ear-to-ear grins of satisfaction.

Is There More That the Internet Offers?

Another really great feature of the information superhighway is that you can communicate with other people all over the world at the cost of a local phone call. I remember when we would call my grandparents and have just enough time to say, "Hello. How are things?" before my grandfather would say, "Okay. Enough, ladies. This is long distance. Say goodbye now." I don't mean to make light of the cost of a telephone call or how hard my grandfather worked for his money, but wasn't that why they invented long distance, so we could talk to each other? Well, thank heaven for computer technology. I have students who communicate with friends and family across the globe on a daily basis. If it weren't for the Internet, this would be financially impossible for most of us.

E-mail = ?

E-mail, or electronic mail, is the same idea as sending a letter (now lovingly referred to as snail mail), but rather than waiting for it to go from a mailbox to your local post office, get sorted, sent to another post office and then delivered by foot to the recipient, you send your message through the computer and your phone line. This all happens in a matter of seconds rather than days. The reason that it costs only as much as a local phone call is that the e-mail is sent over your telephone wires, through a local, not long distance, phone number.

Was that a bit confusing? Well, it confused me too until I could actually see how it all worked. So if things in this book get a bit murky, have faith that when you get in front of a computer and see what I'm talking about, it will all make sense.

What Else Can a Computer Do for Me?

It cannot be denied that along with all the other things you can accomplish on a computer, it is the Internet, with its access to the "information superhighway," that has made computers a "must-have" in the last few years.

However, having a computer offers you much more than the Internet. You will have the ability to organize your address book, create a family newsletter and, if you want to, simulate flying a plane and master chess. Some of my students track their frequent flier miles, inventory their collectibles and design their own stationery. The computer can consolidate your paperwork, create order in your life and track your finances.

There is no end to how a computer can organize, simplify and enhance your life. But first you need to learn a bit more about computers, decide what you want to buy and get it up and running. The whole undertaking of buying a computer can seem very overwhelming, but

66 I'm sure when my son gave me the computer he thought I might never use it. I guess I wasn't sure either. But I've always been a tinkerer, and the computer became a new challenge. Last month I gave my son advice about web sites to check out for buying a new car. That felt good.99
—Peter

don't get discouraged. This book will guide you through the entire process. You will be pleasantly surprised by how easy it will be to make an educated purchase and how quickly you will learn to use and love your computer.

In Conclusion

Mom now e-mails almost every day. When she and I traveled together to Asia last year, she came equipped with printouts from each country's travel and tourism web sites, weather maps and up-to-date currency charts. All things she found surfing the web.

This world that you keep hearing about is not passing you by—it's just waiting for you to come along. What computers can offer you is amazing and boundless, but you're not alone if it seems elusive and intimidating. Most of my students are over 65, and I can't explain to you how exciting it is for them (and me) when they start to zoom around the Internet.

Before you know it, the world will be your oyster. Trust me, if my mother can do it, you can too! (I'm only teasing you, Mom.)

"The computer is such a part of my grandchildren's lives—I wanted to know what it was about. Once I got online, they started to send me weekly e-mails. We used to see one another only at holidays and talk only on birthdays. It's the last thing I expected, but it has brought us closer together."

—Jon

2 Hardware: The Thigh Bone's Connected to the . . .

A simple introduction to the parts of a computer and how they relate to one another

D o you remember the first time you got behind the wheel of a car when you were sixteen? You weren't concerned with how the engine worked or what all the parts were called. What was important was that you learned to drive yourself to the movies (without crashing into anything). The same can be said for the computer. The focus should not be on how it works but on how to get where you want to go.

Computers are very much like cars—they come in different sizes, styles and colors, but they all have the same basic components and do the same thing. A car under your control gets you from one place to another. By performing the tasks you command, a computer gets you from one piece of information to another. In the same way that you decide where to go for a Sunday drive, you decide where to go on the computer and, before long, you'll enjoy yourself along the way. But first let's get familiar with the machine.

The Hardware of the Computer

Hardware is the machinery of the computer. Whatever your motivation is to learn how to use a computer, the basic parts of the machine and what they do will be the same for everyone. You do *not* need to understand how the parts of a computer work in order to use a computer, but it can be helpful to know what they are called. Just read through the information below and know that it is here for you to refer to if you need it later.

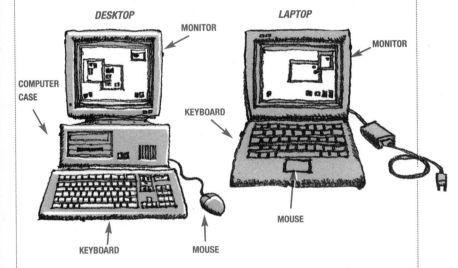

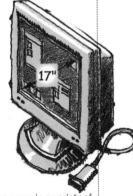

The Monitor

The monitor is a box that contains the screen of the computer. Its function is as you would guess. It is where any information in your computer is viewed. For example, as you type a letter using the keyboard of your computer, the words will appear on the screen of your monitor.

You can get monitors in as many different sizes as you can buy television sets. The monitor size is measured in

Monitors come in a variety of styles and sizes, includiing this flat-panel model.

> ❝*I have an enormous family, and come Christmas my computer is my personal assistant. It keeps a list of who I sent cards to and who I get them from. It also keeps track of what gifts I gave to my 13(!) grandchildren and, of course, who has been naughty and who has been nice.*❞
> —Joan

diagonal inches from a top corner to the opposite bottom corner of the screen itself. For most, bigger is better. When we narrow down what is the best computer for you, we'll talk more about screen options.

The Mouse

A mouse is basically a hand-operated device that controls the movement of a pointer that appears on your monitor's screen. This pointer can appear in different shapes depending on what its function is at a given time. It can also be referred to as the arrow, mouse arrow or cursor.

A mouse can come in a variety of shapes and sizes, but all perform in the same way. You rest your hand or finger on the mouse, and when you move your hand, a ball on the bottom of the mouse moves. When the ball on the bottom of the mouse moves, it sends a message through a cable to the brain of the computer, and the pointer or arrow on your screen moves accordingly. You press and release a button (or buttons) on the top of the mouse to perform an action. A slight click can be heard when you do this, so people often refer to the motion as "clicking the mouse."

Sometime in the 1970s, Xerox researchers invented computer icons. Icons are pictures on your computer screen that you click on to take an action rather than typing in a text command. Shortly afterwards a device was created that would move about on tiny wheels to control the clicking action used to activate icons. The original name for the

The mouse controls the pointer that appears on the computer screen. You can choose from among several types of mouse styles.

66The hardest part for me was learning to use the mouse. I never thought I would figure it out. But I kept practicing and making mistakes and practicing some more. It isn't quite second nature yet, but I'm getting there.99
—Martin

mouse was "X-Y position indicator for a display system." What a mouthful! It didn't take long for the little gray device with the long tail (a cord connected to the computer) to be renamed a mouse. Eureka!

The Keyboard

The keyboard on a computer is very similar to the keyboard on a typewriter. The alphabet and number keys are set up in exactly the same pattern as on your old Smith-Corona and function in the same way. Whatever you type on the keyboard will appear on your monitor's screen.

However, the computer keyboard is not used just for typing. There are several other keys beyond the numbers and the letters, such as arrow keys that allow you to move around the screen, much as you do with the mouse. There is either an **Enter** key, on a PC, or **Return** key, on a Mac, as well as some additional keys that are called function keys.

The Enter and Return keys are significant because through them you can instruct the computer to carry out a task. These keys are similar to the addition and subtraction keys on a calculator. With a computer you can depress a keyboard key to tell the computer to move a paragraph, delete a sentence or access a piece of information. *A word of caution:* You don't want to use the Enter or Return keys without knowing what the result will be. Enough said on that. It is hard to visualize this without having a computer in front of you. You'll see what I mean when you start working with an actual keyboard.

Even though the mouse and keyboard are physically very different, there are many functions that can be carried out by using either of them. For example, if you want to move from the top to the bottom of a page, you can use either the keyboard or the mouse to get the job done. When you are on the

A computer keyboard is set up much like a standard typewriter, with additional keys that perform specific tasks.

Internet, most of your activity will be controlled by the mouse, but the keyboard will remain essential for typing information.

The monitor, keyboard and mouse are the most straightforward parts of a computer. Each of them plays a major role in allowing you to view, access and manipulate information.

One other thing is worth mentioning: I don't know how to type. As a student described it, I use the "Columbus Method"—find the key and land on it. I am sharing this with you in case you think that you can't use a computer if you don't know how to type. Poppycock. It's how I make my living.

The Brain of the Computer

There are several components that make up the brain of the computer, all of which work together to gather, identify, move and store information.

The computer case houses the "brain" of the computer. Cases come in various shapes and sizes. This vertical box is called a tower case.

The Computer Case

A computer case is nothing more than a plastic box, but it houses the most important and most expensive part of your computer—the central processing unit (CPU), the hard drive (C:) and the random access memory (RAM). Sounds complicated already, doesn't it? Fear not. This combination of CPU, hard drive and RAM is simply the brain of your machine. Some users refer to the computer case as a BUB (big ugly box). I could not have said it better myself.

The Central Processing Unit (CPU) is the pathway for all of the information in your computer. The CPU is to information on the computer what the post office is to a letter. The information has to go through the CPU to get to its proper place. When you hear references to *megahertz*, people are

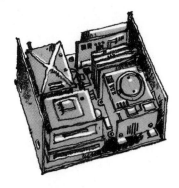

A peek inside a standard computer case . . . eek!

talking about the speed of the CPU, or how quickly it moves information through your computer. The more megahertz, the faster the computer will operate. It's not unlike your car—the more horsepower it has, the faster it goes from 0 to 60.

The Hard Drive (C: Drive) is the permanent memory of your computer. The information that you type into the computer lives on the hard drive, as does the software that has been installed. (I'll explain software in the next chapter.) Even when your computer is turned off, the information remains stored in the hard drive.

Random Access Memory (RAM) is the memory used to open up programs or images only while the computer is on. The size of the RAM is important when we get on the Internet. Web sites are made up of pictures, and to help those pictures appear on the screen, your computer uses the power of the RAM.

In summary, the CPU is the organizer and messenger of all information in the computer. The hard drive and RAM both store information. The hard drive is your permanent memory, and RAM is the temporary memory used only when the computer is on.

The Brain's Memory

Information stored in a computer takes up space. This space is measured in bytes. Both the hard drive and the RAM are measured in bytes.

• A **megabyte** can store about as much text as *Moby Dick*.
• A **gigabyte** is capable of storing about 1,000 copies of *Moby Dick*.

So if you're planning to write a fat book about a whale and follow up with 999 sequels, you'll want a computer with a hard drive of at least a gigabyte! I'll explain how many bytes you'll really need for your hard drive and RAM when we're closer to shopping for your machine.

How Does It Measure Up?

Hertz (or Megahertz) is a measurement of speed. The CPU (central processing unit) has a speed measured in hertz—the more (i.e., faster) the better.

Bytes (Mega or Giga) is a measurement of space. The hard drive and the RAM (random access memory) are storage spaces measured in bytes—the more the better.

Don't get bogged down if you don't quite grasp the concept of bytes or hertz. It's not necessary to understand either one to use the computer.

Other Parts of the Computer

Here we will review some other essential parts of the computer. Each of the components described in this section transfers information onto the brain of the computer.

A: and D: Drives

As I said before, the hard drive, also sometimes referred to as the C: drive, is where all information is permanently stored on your computer. The A: and D: drives (on some computers the D: drive is referred to as the E: drive) are where information can be fed or "installed" into the computer.

A:

D:

The A: drive is where a floppy disk is inserted. The D: drive is for a CD-ROM.

A floppy disk is inserted into the A: drive in the same way you put a cassette tape into a car stereo. A CD-ROM is inserted into the D: drive in the same way you put a CD into a compact disc player.

This is all theoretical at the moment, but when you get near a computer, whether it's in a store, at a friend's or at your local library, take a look at the A: and D: drives. You'll see that it's really quite simple.

Modem

A modem is a device that connects your computer to your telephone line, which in turn connects your computer to the outside world. This allows you to access the Internet and send e-mail. You *cannot* access the Internet or send e-mail without a modem.

All computers come with a floppy drive and/or CD-ROM drive. Without at least one of these drives, you would have no way to install software onto your computer. Because software can be found in both formats (floppy and CD-ROM), I recommend you get a computer with both types of drives.

A modem can be either internal or external. Most computers have a modem inside the computer case, along with the CPU, hard drive and RAM. Older computers may require an external modem, which is a separate piece of machinery that plugs into the back of the computer case. Whether it is internal or external, a telephone line is plugged into the modem and the other end of the phone line is plugged into your phone jack.

Modems come in different speeds. The speed of the modem will affect how quickly or slowly transmission happens over the phone line. With a fast modem, your e-mail or an image on the Internet arrives more quickly. A fast modem, even if it is a bit more expensive, relieves you of the frustration of waiting and waiting for information to appear on the computer's screen. (World Wide Web, a.k.a. World Wide Wait.)

You don't need to have an extra telephone number installed for a modem. It can share the same line as your present phone, but while you're on the Internet, anyone who calls you will get a busy signal. I have a separate phone line because I like to be able to call friends while I'm surfing the net. However, there are also cable lines now on the market that won't tie up your phone line while you're on the Internet.

The monitor, like the keyboard and mouse, is connected to the computer case by a cable.

How Does It All Get Connected?

Let's review the hardware on a computer before we get into how it is connected. There is a monitor, mouse and keyboard. There is also the computer case, which houses the brain of the computer, the modem and the disk drives. The pieces of hardware must be connected in order to have information conveyed from one part to another.

Ports

On the back of the computer case you will see a bunch of "ports." Ports are where the cords that connect each piece

The cables that connect the various parts of the computer are plugged into ports in the back of the computer case. Thank heaven the ports have different shapes. It makes plugging them in a whole lot easier.

of hardware to the computer case are plugged in. For example, the monitor must be connected before you can view the information that your computer has stored. The connection between the monitor and the computer case is made by way of a port. A cable coming from the back of the monitor is plugged into a port on the computer case. The same is true for the keyboard, mouse and any additional equipment you may choose to have, such as a printer. On the computer case there is also a place to plug in an electrical cord to bring electricity to the computer.

Anything that uses the brain of the computer to function needs to be plugged into the computer case. Each piece of hardware has a differently shaped plug to match a specific port. This makes it difficult to plug things in incorrectly, which, thankfully, makes connecting the parts of a computer easier than you would expect.

Peripherals

Peripherals are pieces of hardware that you can add to your computer above and beyond the basic pieces of hardware discussed. These can be added at any time, so there is no

"With every e-mail from my kids that I print out for my mother, she gets closer and closer to wanting a computer of her own."
—Evelyn

Printers, like the two here, are designed in a variety of styles and sizes.

urgency to buy them when you make your computer purchase. But a printer is pretty essential and I think you'll regret not having one from the get-go.

Printer

The printer will print whatever you ask it to print from the computer. For example, you can print the letters or recipes that you've written or an e-mail that you've received. You can also print the information from the web sites that you've pulled up on the Internet. Perhaps you have accessed a web site that allows you to order airline tickets and shows the seating plan of the plane. Before you order the tickets, you might print out the seating plan so that you and the folks traveling with you can decide which seats you would like.

Scanner

A scanner is a bit like a photocopier. It scans an image and sends a copy of that image to your computer. Once the image is in your computer, you can make changes to it, print it or even send it as e-mail. I have a student who is building a new house. She scanned her first pictures of the construction crew's progress into her computer. Then she wrote an e-mail to each of her children and attached the pictures to the e-mails so they could see the house. It was really exciting and not very hard to do.

A flat-bed scanner.

A scanner can also scan documents. This same student scans all her bank statements into her computer. She still has access to the information, but it isn't taking up all that room in her file cabinet.

Don't fret if you feel overwhelmed by the technical aspect of this information. How many of us can actually describe how our toaster works? Do you have any problem using a toaster? I don't think so!

A combination printer, scanner and copier.

A: drive the place to insert floppy disks

arrow keys features of the keyboard; allow movement of the cursor around the screen

bytes measurement of space

CD-ROM contains software to be installed onto the computer

click depressing the mouse button to take an action

computer case contains the CPU, hard drive, RAM, modem and disk drives

CPU (central processing unit) the processing part of the computer

D: drive (or E: drive) the place to insert CD-ROMs

Enter or Return and function keys features of the keyboard; perform actions

floppy disk contains software to be installed onto the computer (can also be used to copy information from your computer)

hard drive (or C: drive) where information is permanently stored

hertz measurement of speed

keyboard used to type information into the computer

modem communicates through a phone line to connect to the Internet

monitor houses the screen where information is viewed

mouse device to move the pointer on the screen

peripherals additional pieces of hardware such as a printer or scanner attached to the computer

pointer appears on the screen and moves according to the manipulation of the mouse; also referred to as the arrow, mouse arrow or cursor

port where cords that connect the different computer parts are plugged in

printer allows you to print information from the computer

RAM (random access memory) temporary memory used when the computer is on

scanner copies images and text into the computer

3 Software: Feeding the Computer Brain

An explanation of software and how it is used

In order for a computer to function, it must have software added to the brain. Without software, a computer is nothing more than an oversized paperweight. Think of it this way: Hardware is the machinery and brain of the computer. The machinery and brain are useless unless information is added to it. Software is the information. It's like the telephone: The phone is the hardware; our voices are the software. You do *not* need to completely understand software to be able to use a computer. Again, the goal is to be able to use the computer, not dismantle it.

Operating Software *vs.* Application Software

There are two types of software—operating software and application software. Your computer will come with operating software already stored on the hard drive. (Remember, the hard drive is the permanent memory of the computer.)

Operating software organizes and manages your computer. Think of it as the computer's filing system and library.

In Chapter 2 we became familiar with the central processing unit (CPU)—the hardware that organizes the flow of information. Well, the operating software works hand in hand with the CPU. A computer would not be able to function without operating software. It would be like having the lumber (hardware) to make a house, but no foundation and no blueprints (operating software).

Application software, with the help of the operating software, enables you to perform certain tasks (e.g., type a letter, design a web site, chart your family genealogy). For example, word-processing application software allows you to use the computer as a typewriter with advanced editing tools. Other application software teaches you to speak Spanish, set up your taxes or simulate piloting a plane. There are thousands of different application software programs on the market.

Why Can't I Stick with My Old Underwood?

If you make a mistake on a typewriter, you have to remove the error with correction tape or Wite Out or, even worse, type it all again. With a computer you can make tons of changes on a document and view it in its entirety on the screen to make sure it's just the way you want it before you print it out. The computer will even check the spelling and grammar for you.

Different Kinds of Application Software

Word Processing	lets you type and edit letters, recipes, a novel
Financial Management	helps you track accounts, print checks, pay bills
Organizational	helps you maintain a calendar, address book, home inventory
Communication	enables you to send faxes and mail, travel the Internet
Educational	offers you typing instruction, languages, reference materials
Graphics	lets you create pictures and design cards, invitations
Entertainment	games, games, games

How Does the Software Get into the Computer?

Software needs to be transferred to the brain of the computer. This is done by way of a CD-ROM or a floppy disk. The CD-ROM and floppy disk drives of the computer read the information off these disks and store it in the brain. The CD-ROM and floppy disk drives are the bridge between software and the computer.

Floppy Disks and CD-ROMs

Regardless of which type of application software interests you, it will come in the form of either a floppy disk or a CD-ROM. A floppy disk (also called a diskette) is about the same size, shape and weight as a square coaster, 4″ × 4″, and it isn't floppy at all. It was named for the original disk that came out decades ago, which was larger and would flop if you held it by a corner and snapped your wrist. Nowadays floppy disks are smaller, made of sturdy plastic and are much more durable.

A CD-ROM looks just like a compact disc for a stereo. However, unlike a compact disc for your stereo, which contains only sound, a CD-ROM is capable of holding sound, text and images (even moving images), which we can access on our computer's monitor and speakers. A CD-ROM can also store the equivalent of an entire set of encyclopedias, about 400 times the information on a floppy.

It used to be that a CD-ROM drive was considered a luxury add-on, but this is no longer the case. While it is still possible to buy a computer without one, I wouldn't advise it. Why? More and more software is being offered *only* on CD-ROM. In some cases, the manufacturer has to be

Both CD-ROMs (left) and floppy disks (above) store information. A CD-ROM stores 400 times as much as a floppy.

contacted directly to get their software on floppy disks. Also because a CD-ROM stores so much more than a floppy, it may require several floppy disks to get the same job done as one CD-ROM. In short, a CD-ROM is easier, more convenient and, now, more widely used.

Installing Software

Before you can use application software, it needs to be added to the brain of the computer. To add software to your computer, your computer transfers the information stored on a floppy disk or CD-ROM onto the hard drive. This process of transferring the software to the hard drive is referred to as "installing" software. Once the software has been installed, it is stored permanently on the hard drive.

To install software, you first insert either the floppy disk or CD-ROM into its proper drive (see the illustration to the left). If it's a floppy disk it will be inserted into the A: drive of the computer case, label side up, metal end first. After part of the floppy disk has been inserted into the A: drive, it sort of snaps into place all by itself. You don't need to use any force.

The D: drive for the CD-ROM works slightly differently. There is a button you push to have the D: drive open. What looks like a shallow cup holder in your car will slide out. You will place the CD-ROM on this tray, label side up, and push the button again to close the tray. This particular piece of the computer can be quite fragile. *You never want to force the CD-ROM tray to close. Always use the open and close button.*

Once the disk is inserted, you will either follow the written instructions included with the software or the instructions that will appear on the screen of your computer. Through this process the hard drive will transfer and store the information from the floppy or CD-ROM into the brain of the computer. You may also hear people refer to this transferring of data as "reading" the software onto the computer.

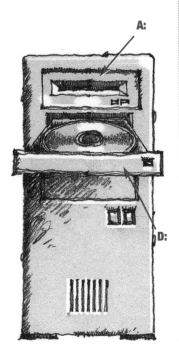

A:

D:

A floppy disk is inserted into the A: drive. A CD-ROM is inserted into the D: drive. Once the disk is inserted, the computer can read the contents.

How Else Can a Floppy Disk or CD-ROM Be Used?

We've discussed putting information into the computer, but what if you want to take information out of the computer? A floppy disk can work in two ways. Information can be transferred from the floppy disk onto the computer. The reverse is also true; you can take information from the computer and store it on a floppy disk.

Let's say that you want to give your publisher a copy of the autobiography you've typed on the computer. You could print out the whole book and lug it to the publisher's office. Or you could copy it onto a blank floppy disk, slip the disk into your pocket and stroll over to deliver it. At that point your publisher would install the information from the floppy disk onto the hard drive of their computer.

On an older computer the CD-ROM is a one-way operation. Information can be transferred from a CD-ROM onto your computer, but the old ones do not let you transfer information onto the CD-ROM. Now there are "writeable" CD-ROM drives on the market that allow information to be transferred onto them.

Upgrading Software

As you purchase your new software, a group of diligent computer researchers (a.k.a. computer geeks) are fast at work improving that software. So within a relatively short period of time, there may be a new and improved version of what you have purchased. This is true for application and operating software. Both are constantly being improved and changed to better meet your needs. It may be that the upgrade is just cosmetic, or that the company corrected glitches people complained about. Rather than buying a

Where to Buy Software

Mail-Order Catalogs
- Often have the best prices.
- Generally have well-informed salespeople.
- Be sure to ask if they have a money-back guarantee!

Software Stores
- Competitive prices.
- The good ones have informed salespeople.
- Face-to-face contact.
- Generally have a fair return policy, but do check it out.

Online
- You can often sample the software on your computer.
- Can be purchased and transferred from the Internet onto your hard drive.
- You won't be given a manual.

Pirating
- Accepting unauthorized copies of software is unlawful.
- You will not get technical support from the manufacturer.

Register Your Goods

It is important that you fill out and send in your product registration information on your software. This is the way the manufacturer can reach you to notify you of an upgrade in their product, and it may be for free!

whole new version of the software, you can buy an upgrade from the manufacturer. Some manufacturers offer their upgrades at a greatly reduced price; others may offer it for free.

An upgrade comes in the form of either a floppy disk or a CD-ROM and is installed on the computer as you would install any application software. Once you install the upgrade, it will automatically make changes to the existing software on your hard drive to reflect the improvements.

You do not need to upgrade your software unless you need to or want to. When the time comes, you will know whether you are interested in the improvements that are being touted.

When purchasing software, look to buy from a company that isn't going to disappear into the sunset. Buy only from a manufacturer with a good reputation and a solid track record.

■ LET'S REVIEW

application software lets you perform specialized tasks, such as word processing

CD-ROM used to install software onto the computer

floppy disk used to install software onto the computer and to copy information from your computer

installing process where software is read and stored on the hard drive

operating software the system that organizes and manages your computer

upgrade new and improved generation of an existing software program

"writeable" CD-ROM functions like the CD-ROM, but can also copy information from your computer

Where Will It Sleep and How Often Do I Need to Water It?

There Is No Place Like Home vs. Taking Your Show on the Road

Desktop vs. laptop

Can you picture yourself sitting in your backyard watching the roses bloom while "surfing the net"? Or perhaps you're traveling on a plane with your computer tucked into your carry-on luggage. On the other hand, maybe you're sure you'll use the computer only in the warmth of your den and have no intention of moving it. This chapter will help you decide whether a desktop or laptop best suits your needs, based on how you think you might want to use it. If at the end of this chapter you're still on the fence, don't lose hope; we'll be test-driving the options after Chapter 8.

Desktop and laptop computers do the same things. The main difference is size.

How Are Desktops and Laptops Alike?

First, let's discuss the similarities. A desktop and a laptop function in exactly the same way, using the same software and allowing you to access the Internet. They both have the same basic hardware (monitor, keyboard and mouse) and they think alike—using the CPU (central processing unit), hard drive and RAM (random access

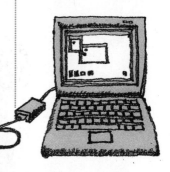

Keeping the Battery Charged

A laptop computer's battery recharges when you plug the machine into an electrical outlet, not unlike your DustBuster. The computer doesn't need to be turned on to recharge (but your surge protector does). For maximum battery life, you should let the battery fully run down every month.

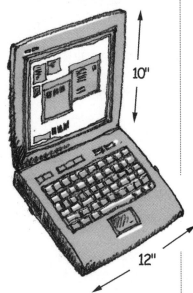

10"

12"

The average laptop is about the same size as a small stack of magazines and weighs between 4 and 7 pounds. There are some swankier designs that are even smaller and lighter.

memory). Both use the A: drive to read floppy disks and the D: drive to read CD-ROMs. Software is installed on both types of computers in the same manner. They also have the capability of being linked to a printer or other peripherals using ports. (If these parts of the computer are still vague, just look over the "Let's Review" section at the end of Chapters 2 and 3 to refresh your memory.)

How Is a Laptop Different from a Desktop?

Laptops aren't so very different from desktop computers. Laptops were given their name because they are small enough and light enough to sit comfortably on your lap when you use them. A laptop can also be referred to as a "notebook" because it's just about the same size as a notebook. To be realistic, most laptop (or notebook) computers are a little too big and heavy to slip under your arm as you would a real notebook, but they do get smaller and lighter every year. There are no cables connecting the monitor, keyboard and mouse on a laptop because these parts are all contained within the laptop.

The sacrifice that you make for something so portable is that everything is smaller. Both the monitor and keyboard on a laptop are smaller than on a desktop—in fact, you may find the laptop screen difficult to view. And if your hands are large, you may feel cramped using the keyboard or mouse. But for some people it is infinitely more important that they can take the computer with them, even if it is a little less comfortable to use. Read on—there are some other things to consider.

Freedom of Movement

Laptops can be plugged into a wall outlet or they can run off a battery. On average, laptops run for about two hours on a fully charged battery. This is wonderful for people who want to use a computer while en route and don't have access to a wall outlet. Another battery bonus: If you are plugged into a wall outlet and you lose electricity, the machine won't shut down (potentially losing the document you are working on). Instead, the battery will kick in automatically and the computer will keep going and going and . . .

The Cost of Freedom

The weight of laptop computers varies. The lightest one out now is about 2 pounds, but most average about 6 pounds and may be too heavy to carry around for very long. Remember, when you transport your computer, you will also have to take along the electrical adapter, cord and case, all of which add weight.

There are other possible disadvantages to taking your computer with you. You risk dropping it, losing it or having it stolen. To be on the safe side, my laptop is covered under my renter's policy in case it disappears while I'm on the road.

Space Saving/Visual Appeal

A laptop may appeal to you even if you're not thinking of traveling with it. It will take up less space in your home than a desktop computer. There is a big difference between the look of a monitor, keyboard and bulky computer case with all their messy cable attachments and that of a box the size of a small stack of magazines.

Mouse Types for a Laptop

A desktop comes with a standard external mouse. This is not true of a laptop. Laptops usually come with either a

66 Within a few months we both loved the computer so much that we decided to buy a laptop so we could take it with us when we travel and so when we're home we don't fight over whose turn it is to use the desktop computer! 99
—Marie and Larry

touchpad or a touchpoint. You won't necessarily be able to choose which type of mouse will be on your laptop.

Unlike a desktop computer, a laptop doesn't have an external mouse. A laptop mouse is usually either a touch-pad (left) or touch-point (right).

Some manufacturers have just one type of mouse, and others offer a choice. If you're interested in purchasing a laptop, it is vital that you try out each type of mouse to see how it feels. By no means should you expect to find it easy to manipulate any of these mouse options without practice, but you may favor one over the other by its feel. Be assured you will be able to use whichever mouse you choose with great dexterity over time.

Expense

At the moment laptops are more expensive than desktops. Smaller parts = more technology = more $$$. Over time this may level off. There is a waiting game that some people play with computers: "If I wait long enough, will they get cheaper?" The answer is probably yes, but as long as you shop wisely, it is possible to buy something now and not feel like a fool in a few years (or months!).

Answers: 1. Laptop 2. Laptop 3. Desktop 4. Laptop 5. Desktop 6. Desktop

Having Said All This . . .

I didn't mean to hold out on you, but I wanted you to really weigh your basic options before I tell you how you can have it both ways. If you want to buy a laptop because it's portable, but you're concerned about the comfort of working on a laptop while at home, you could plug a larger monitor and a standard keyboard into your laptop through ports in the back of the machine for home use. And if you don't like the mouse on your laptop, you can even attach an external mouse.

It is possible to attach an external mouse, keyboard and/or monitor to a laptop so you can enjoy the larger features of a desktop.

There is another rarely used option available that combines a portable computer (a laptop or notebook) and a desktop computer—it's called a "docking station." With a docking station you slide your laptop into a computer case, thus accessing all the power and parts of the station. When you want to venture out with the laptop, you just remove it from the docking station and off you go. This option is expensive, and for most of us it is unnecessary.

You may now know which type of computer (laptop or desktop) is best for you. But if you don't, have no fear. Once you've seen and touched a variety of computers, you will instinctively feel what is right for you. Just keep reading and we'll get there together. For those of you who already know what kind you want to buy, stick with us—there's still more to consider.

5 Selecting Your Workspace
Tips on finding a comfortable and safe work area

Some people have the luxury of an entire room dedicated to their computer; others need to be more resourceful. One of my students whose space is limited converted a closet into a small home office; she opens the closet door and pulls up a chair to work on the computer. Another student utilizes an old armoire. When she's done working she just closes the doors and her "little secret" is hidden in the living room. There are many factors that affect your decision in selecting the best place to set up your computer. Setting up shop inside an extra closet may work for one person but may not be very pleasant for another.

Assuming that you can use the dining room table and move all your things in time for dinner isn't realistic. Using that spare storage room may seem like a great idea, but if you leave all those musty boxes in there with you, you're probably not going to want to spend much time there either. Take a few minutes to stroll around your home. Scan the space for possible work areas. Ideally, where you put your computer will be a space where you like to be.

The Three Little Bears Test

Set a chair where you think you might like to put your computer workstation. Sit in the chair for a bit—read a chapter of this book, check out the sports section or browse a magazine. Does the space feel right to you? Is it too noisy? Is it too drafty? Or is it just right?

What You Need to Check Out

Some desktop computers are designed so that the monitor sits on top of the computer case.

You'll want to choose a spot near an electrical outlet and a phone jack. If your setup is not near an electrical outlet, you will end up with extension cords for the computer, as well as whatever peripherals you may buy, snaking all over the floor.

You will need a phone jack for your modem. This is true whether your modem is internal or external. It is also handy to have a phone near the computer in case you need to call for technical assistance. If there is no phone jack where you want to set up the computer, you can have one installed or you can run a long phone cord from the nearest jack to your modem.

The Computer Desk

Tower computer cases are designed to stand vertically under a desk.

Even though a laptop is smaller than a desktop, it, too, needs a happy and safe home. One of my students confessed that she sits on the sofa with her computer on her lap while watching television. (It *is* called a laptop, isn't it?) This is fine every once in a while, but even a laptop should have a designated work area. It will make your time at the computer more efficient and enjoyable.

If your computer is a desktop, you'll need a table or desk large enough to hold the computer case, monitor and keyboard. Make sure there is space so the computer case can be positioned within reach (not a big stretch) from where you will sit. You don't want to have to get out of your seat to insert a floppy disk or CD-ROM.

If you are short of space, you might want to consider a tower computer case instead of a standard one (see illustration to the left). Tower computer cases stand vertically and can fit under a desk, thereby saving a great deal of desktop space. Whether you choose a laptop or a

It's important to set your computer up properly to avoid strain or injury.

desktop, you'll also need to have enough empty space on your desk to fit a book or any papers you might refer to while you're at the computer.

A standard desk is usually too high for proper computer posture. Ideally, your thighs should be at about a 90-degree angle to your calves and, with your hands resting on the keyboard, your elbows should be at a 90-degree angle as well. This can be solved in three different ways:

1. If possible, adjust the height of your chair to put your body higher than you would normally sit at the desk. Unfortunately, this may cramp your leg space.

2. Invest in a computer desk or workstation. Not only is it designed to accommodate peripherals (such as your printer), thereby giving you a single unit where all the parts of your computer can be together, but your keyboard will be at the proper height in a holder attached below the desk top. The position of the keyboard is significant because you will prevent wrist injury when you maintain a straight line from elbow to fingertips.

A retractable keyboard shelf fits under a desk or computer table.

3. If you don't want to invest in a special computer desk, you can buy just a keyboard holder that can be installed under your current desk. This will put the keyboard at a healthier height and free up more desk space.

You don't have to have your computer space set up perfectly in the beginning. I'm just letting you know that the more you use the computer, the more you'll have to be careful not to strain yourself in any way. If all you have at the moment is a card table in the corner of your living room, start there. My computer is set up on an antique tea cart in my dining room with the printer on the shelf below. I use a dining room chair with two pillows on it. Because this is not the best arrangement for my back, I make sure to get up and walk around every half hour or so.

Some Other Things You Need to Consider

There are health issues that should not be ignored with regard to choosing where you set up your computer. "Ergonomically correct" is a phrase becoming almost as

Watch your posture and your distance from the screen. Your elbows, knees and hips should be at 90-degree angles.

popular as "politically correct." It refers to creating a healthy work environment and positioning your body properly to accomplish the task at hand without injury.

Monitor: Your monitor should be at a 15-degree angle below your sight line. If you set the monitor on the computer case, that may or may not bring it to the correct height. If it doesn't, try setting the monitor on a large phone book or a dictionary instead. Be sure that the monitor is stable.

To avoid eyestrain, it is essential to properly position the monitor.

15°

Chair: The chair you sit on is extremely important. You need to make sure that you have proper back support. If you want to make the investment, an adjustable office chair is the best choice. Used office furniture can often be found through your local classified section.

Footrest: You also want to make sure you don't cut off circulation in the back of your legs. If you need to raise your feet, an open file drawer, a wastebasket or a couple of books make great, inexpensive footrests.

Glasses: If you wear glasses (especially bifocals), you may want to visit your eye doctor to be sure your prescription will be accurate for the computer. I have

To avoid wrist strain, keep a straight line from your elbow to your fingertips.

It is recommended by the National Institute of Occupational Safety and Health that you take at least one 15-minute break for every hour that you are at the computer. You need to relax your eyes and move your body a bit. Something as simple as going to the kitchen to get a drink of water is enough to ease strain.

several students who have a separate pair of glasses that they use exclusively for the computer.

Keyboard: Your keyboard should be at a height where your elbows are at a 90-degree angle and there is an unbroken line from your wrist to your fingertips. Try adding a cushion to your chair, if you need to sit higher.

Injuring yourself while sitting at a computer may seem a bit odd to you, but it's not uncommon. Bad posture, repetitive motion and eyestrain can take a real toll. Many people lose track of time when they're in front of a computer. Before they know it, they've been staring at the screen for two solid hours without ever moving their body from its slightly slumped position.

Your equipment manuals give sound advice about proper computer ergonomics. We will review safety issues again when you are actually using the computer.

A Few Don'ts

Besides making sure you're physically comfortable at the computer, there are a few potential problems to avoid when setting things up.

Don't place the computer in too tight a space. A computer generates a fair amount of heat, and you want to make sure that air can circulate around it.

Don't place the computer by an open window. The glare from the sun may make it difficult to view the screen. Also, constant direct sunlight on the computer can make the computer too warm when in use. And, all of the microscopic things that blow in the window (whether it is grit in New York City or pollen in Nebraska) can eventually damage the inner workings of the computer.

Don't let your animals get too friendly with your computer. Cats in particular are attracted to the heat emitted by the computer case and monitor. Unfortunately, animal fur can really muck up your system.

Don't put your computer equipment in a room with thick carpeting. Very thick carpeting can conduct excessive static electricity, which can be harmful to the computer. If you choose to get a tower computer case, *do not* set it directly on carpeting. There are trays you can buy to hold it, or simply set it on a wooden board.

Don't place any magnets near the computer or the software. Magnets have been known to damage the monitor and erase the information contained on a floppy disk. Crazy, but true.

Don't place any kind of liquid near the computer. Spilling fluids on the keyboard can cause serious and expensive damage. This includes cereal and milk. I had to have my computer repaired after breakfast didn't make it from the bowl to my mouth. If my computer hadn't still been under warranty, I'd have been crying over spilt milk.

What Else?

You've chosen your work area and decided the best way to arrange everything once you make your purchase. Be sure to measure your workspace before you go computer shopping. Bring the measurements with you and refer to them to ensure a perfect fit.

There is another thing to do to get completely prepared for bringing your new computer home. You will need to have a small amount of easy-access storage space near your work area. A shelf on a bookcase or a file box will do. You'll want to store equipment manuals, floppy disks and CD-ROMs, as well as other office supplies, such as paper and replacement ink cartridges for your printer.

Addressing the issues of your workspace before you go into a store ensures that your computer will have a good home. Now we can get to the business of deciding what kind of computer is right for you.

Go for a Test-Drive

6 Apples and Oranges
Macintosh vs. PC

Perhaps you've decided whether a desktop or a laptop computer best meets your needs. And you've scoped out your home for the perfect place to set up shop. The next big question is— should you buy a Mac or a PC?

The Apple Macintosh computer is referred to as a Mac or an Apple and has, as you have probably seen, a rainbow-clad apple as its logo. Macs were the first computers designed for personal use that used visuals (or icons) as a way to get from one piece of information on the computer to another. They also introduced the mouse and menus (lists of options). These innovations were designed to make the Mac easy and fun to use and less confusing (a.k.a. "user-friendly").

In the 1980s IBM came out with a model called the IBM PC (IBM Personal Computer). For a while people referred to other non-Mac brands as IBM-compatible, but that didn't make for catchy advertising, so the partial name PC (Personal Computer) stuck.

Technically, a Mac is also a personal computer (PC), but it has the prestige of carrying its own brand name. For our purposes a Macintosh is a Mac or an Apple, and a PC is everything else.

What About Clones?

A clone is a computer whose manufacturer has taken the idea of another and created a similar machine. At the moment there are no clones for the Mac. There are, however, many companies that have cloned the original IBM PC and have actually surpassed IBM in sales. Some of the manufacturers' names might be familiar to you: Compaq, Dell, Toshiba, Gateway, among others. Calling these very successful competitors to IBM "clones" doesn't seem quite right, but this is the jargon we still use today. Often companies that have cloned a design have done a great deal of research and made improvements upon the original concept.

What Makes a PC and a Mac So Different?

When the Macintosh hit the market in 1984, the differences between its system and that of the PC were enormous. Mac had an incredibly easy operating system (remember, the operating system is what manages the information you have in your machine) and became known as the company that made computers user-friendly. That translates to ease of use, less intimidating and more fun. They accomplished this through creative graphic design and the use of visual cues to access information on the computer.

Macintosh made the decision not to share its operating system with any other manufacturers. Think of it this way— Macs speak a special language all their own. The pickle is that Macs and PCs have different operating systems. When

"I had no idea that my daughter used a different type of computer than I did. I thought they all worked the same. When I called her in a panic and she couldn't help me, I felt lost. Luckily, my neighbor also has a PC, and he came to my rescue."

—Dan

software is designed, it needs to be designed in one version for Macs to understand and in another version for all other PCs to understand.

When Mac decided *not* to share its operating system, this left the door open for someone else to enter the market. That is exactly what Microsoft did when it came out with Windows 95 (the predecessor to Windows 98 and Windows 2000). Microsoft designed a PC operating system based on a lot of Mac's original ideas. The creation of Windows 95 gave PCs an operating system as straightforward and user-friendly as the Mac's.

At this time PCs dominate the market. There are close to ten PC owners for every Mac owner. If the majority of people are buying software for a PC, naturally, the priority for manufacturers is to create software for the majority. Until recently a lot of computer software came out in a PC version long before the Mac version hit the stores, and in some cases it was never designed for Macs at all. Now,

The Pros and Cons of Macs and PCs

Pros	Cons
Mac	
• used most by graphic designers	• more expensive, but prices are dropping
• still considered more user-friendly	• not always compatible with non-Mac peripherals
• great service record	
PCs	
• less expensive	• design is still catching up to the Mac
• software hits the market first	• operating system can be a bit temperamental
• more brands available	

The ports at the back of an Apple/Mac computer (below) are different from those on a PC.

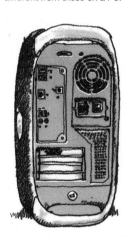

however, there is software that acts as a translator from one operating system to another. It is not perfected yet, but eventually it might make PC software compatible with a Mac.

From a teaching and learning point of view, this translation software would make life so much easier. That way we could all speak the same language. You'll see what I mean later when I describe how to use a computer if you have a PC, then how to use it if you have a Mac. It would be much more efficient to have only one system to explain.

The basic pieces of hardware are the same on both systems. However, the ports where you plug in the monitor, keyboard, printer and other peripherals in the back of the computer case are different. That means that you can't plug a Mac keyboard into a PC computer case and vice versa without some kind of adapter. This is another reason why the division between the two is hard to bridge. You really need to commit to one or the other—they don't mix well.

The dispute between Mac users and PC users is legendary. If you haven't experienced it, just ask Mac users if they would change to a PC, and they will more than likely square their shoulders and give you a powerful *"never."* A PC user might even offer you a knuckle sandwich. I know it sounds ridiculous, but it's true.

Enough Already. Which Should I Buy?

You probably should buy a Mac or a PC based on what your friends and family have—not because you can't march to a different drummer, but because you'll be calling someone you know at 3:00 on a Sunday afternoon when you have a computer problem. If that person has a different operating system than you, his or her ability to advise you will be limited. What if your daughter wants to give you her old monitor or share some software, but she has a Mac and you have a PC? You'll be out of luck.

Don't make a mountain out of a molehill. You will learn to use and love whatever computer you decide to buy. This is a win-win situation. There are more happy PC users in the world than blades of grass in your backyard, and the same is true for Mac users.

■ *LET'S REVIEW*

Mac a brand of personal computer with a unique operating system

clone an old term that once referred to non-IBM PCs

Apple same as a Mac

PC personal computer; used as a name for any computer other than a Mac

Windows 98 or 2000 the operating system used on most PCs

If all your friends have Macs, get a Mac. If they all have PCs, get a PC, but don't limit yourself to purchasing the same brand as all your friends. All PCs work the same way, no matter who manufactured it.

7 Would You Buy a Car Without Test-Driving It?
What to look for when you get behind a keyboard

On more than one occasion I have received calls from students who want me to "choose whatever computer you think is best for me." For the same reasons that it is unwise to buy a car without a test-drive, it is unwise to buy a computer without taking a few different models for a spin. As with a car, you're looking for comfort, ease, speed and quality at the best price possible. How can you know about comfort and ease until you actually touch the machine? Speed and quality, on the other hand, can be determined through research, which includes talking with computer-using friends and family.

What makes one person buy a Cadillac and another a VW bug? I can tell you what kind of computer I like, but my hands may be smaller, my eyesight worse and my needs entirely different from yours. No matter how tempting it is or how much easier it seems, *don't have someone else make your computer-buying decisions for you.* An experienced computer user can give you great advice, but *you* have to get your hands on the machine before you make the final decision. Your adviser is not the one who is going to sit in front of the machine and use it. You are. Would you buy a pair of shoes without trying them on?

> **❝***I was apprehensive about our class field trip to a nearby computer store. It seemed much more than I could handle. But once I tried a couple of different computers, I knew that it was the right thing to do. I still wouldn't stroll into a computer store for fun, but it helped me make a more informed decision.***❞**
>
> **—Carla**

Preparation for Your Test-Drive

Here is a little homework that you need to do *before* you step into a store to test-drive computers:

Try out the computers of your friends and family. Keep in mind that people are usually very loyal to the computer they use and think it is the *only* choice. For your research assignment, the more variety, the better. If no one you know has a computer, go to your local library, senior center or even the high school. I guarantee there will be someone around who is proud of his or her computer skills and eager to show them off.

Do research. An eager salesperson can send you reeling with too much information, so it's best to go into the store with a few computer brands in mind. The salesperson might very well show you a gem that you didn't know about, but you're always better off having done some research on your own.

Look through computer magazines to get an idea of what computers you're interested in seeing. Call the magazine publisher and see which issue has the most recent list of the top ten computers to buy. Get a copy of that issue and narrow your choice to three or four of their top recommendations. Mark the articles so that you remember which computers you want to see. Don't try to read the entire magazine unless you're very interested. It can be confusing (and boring) and may put you off buying a computer.

You might want to call several computer mail-order stores listed in the back of this book. Feel free to ask whatever questions you have. The telephone salespeople are usually very helpful and informative. Give them a call, but do *not* make a purchase yet. It is still important that you go into a store and test-drive different machines—although you may ultimately decide to buy your computer through the mail.

Prepare notes. It's so easy to become confused or forget details. Write down the size of your available workspace, the components you know you're interested in, what information you would like explained and the brands that you want to test-drive. It is a great way to keep organized, and it may make a salesperson stand a little bit more at attention.

In addition to the marked articles, you'll want to take a note like the one at right with you.

Be prepared to take notes. There is nothing worse than spending a whole day shopping for a new apartment or house, seeing a half-dozen possibilities, returning home and not being able to remember one from the other. You definitely don't want to have that happen. There's a form on page 58 that you can use to take down information that you've gathered on your expedition. Later you will be able to review your notes and discuss your choices with others without mixing up the details.

WHAT I WANT MY COMPUTER TO HAVE

MUST-HAVES:
NO LESS THAN 64MB OF RAM, MORE THAN 128MB UNNECESSARY
SCANNER (MAY BE INCLUDED WITH PRINTER)
BARE-BONES WORD-PROCESSING SOFTWARE

QUESTIONS:
IS THERE AN EXTENDED WARRANTY POLICY?
CAN SOMEONE COME TO MY HOUSE AND SET IT UP? HOW MUCH WILL THAT COST?

WORKSPACE:
OLD TEACHER'S DESK WITH SPACE UNDERNEATH—24"HIGH X 30"WIDE

The task at hand is to find out what feels and looks right to you. You are on an information-gathering mission.

If You Haven't Decided between a Desktop or a Laptop . . .

If you still haven't decided which is best for you, go to the computer store solely to help you determine whether you should buy a desktop or a laptop. Try a couple of models of each type. While you're doing so, think again about your workspace and how you're planning to use the machine. Keep in mind that all the basic hardware components are the same on a laptop or a desktop. What you're comparing is how the size of the machine suits your needs and whether you want something portable. Once you've made a choice, leave the store. Either go have lunch and return in the afternoon or come back another day to continue your field trip. This is to be sure that you don't experience information overload. If you feel you've absorbed all you can, take a break. This is an important decision and you want to make a thoughtful choice. If you're still confused after your trip, take another look at the questions in Chapter 4 to help you decide.

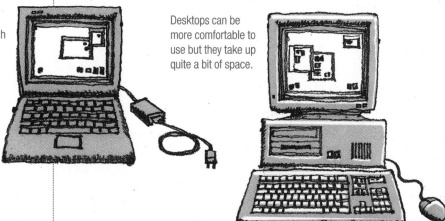

Laptops are portable and don't take up much space but all the components are smaller.

Desktops can be more comfortable to use but they take up quite a bit of space.

It's Only a Test-Drive

Before we prepare for your excursion, I want to make sure you're clear about the purpose of this adventure. Test-driving is not the same as buying. No matter how tempting, *do not buy* your computer the same day that you test-drive. We still have more to learn.

At the end of Chapter 8 you can put this book down and go shopping. My mother has friends who have gone through a whole course of computer lessons at her senior center and still haven't bought a computer because they're intimidated by the computer store. The sad thing is that without a computer to practice on, they have forgotten all that they had learned. Promise yourself that you will go to the store before finishing the entire book. This way you will make the trip, realize it isn't such a big deal and continue learning more about the computer before you make your investment.

You are empowered with knowing this is nothing more than a research expedition. No obligation, no financial outlay, no decision making. If you don't want to go back, there is always the option of mail order or purchasing from the store by phone so that you never have to re-enter the place. And remember, if the salesperson you are dealing with really doesn't appeal to you, give him the brush-off, let him get out of sight, smile sweetly at another salesperson and watch her come running.

Initially the computer store can sometimes add to any confusion you might have, especially after you get home and try to remember all you saw. The Test-Drive Form that follows will give you a written record to reference at your own pace in your own home. You will find an additional form in the back of the book that you can tear out to bring along with you.

> **❝** *I almost skipped class the day of the field trip. It made me think of going to the dentist. But it wasn't that bad at all. I've already gone back twice on my own to ask more questions.* **❞**
> —Catherine

Test-Drive Form

1. **Store:** _____
   Salesperson: _____
   Note the address and phone number of the store and the name of the salesperson you spoke with.

2. **Brand & Model of Computer:** _____
   Include any numbers that follow the brand name—this will indicate the model. For example: Toshiba Satellite 100CS.

3. **Cost:** _____
   Note the basic cost and any additional costs. For example: $1,499 plus $199 for 20MB RAM upgrade = $1,698.

SYSTEM INFORMATION

4. **Computer Case:** ☐ Standard   ☐ Tower
   Is the computer case a standard model or a tower model, which will go on the floor?

5. **CPU Speed:** _____   Upgradeable ☐ Yes ☐ No
   Remember, the CPU speed is measured in megahertz (MHz). You will need a CPU with at least 300MHz, but if you want to splurge, you could go as high as 800MHz, or even higher.

6. **RAM:** _____   Upgradeable ☐ Yes ☐ No
   The RAM size is measured in megabytes (MB). You will want a RAM size of at least 64MB—but 128MB is more fun.

7. **Hard Drive:** _____   Upgradeable ☐ Yes ☐ No
   The hard drive size is also measured in megabytes or gigabytes (GB). I recommend that you start with 6GB. There is no need to exceed 10GB for almost anything you could think of doing on the computer.

8. **Monitor Size:** _____
   Monitor size is measured in diagonal inches from a top corner to the opposite bottom corner of the screen itself. For most, a bigger screen is better, but you can judge what suits you best by checking out several different sizes. A flat-panel screen takes up less space on your desk and has better resolution but is more expensive.

9. **Screen Type:**   Active ☐   Passive ☐

There are two types of screens if you are looking at a laptop with a 13" screen—active and passive. An active screen has a bit more clarity and can be viewed from all angles as clearly as it can straight on. A passive screen can be viewed clearly only from the front. An active screen is substantially more expensive. Make sure you view both types and decide if you think it is worth the extra money for the active screen.

10. **Modem Speed:**_____

Modem speed is measured in kilobytes (KB) per second. Don't linger on this: the higher, the better. If it is included with your computer, the modem will be an internal one. Older machines offer 28KB modems, but most of my students go for a 56KB modem and you should as well. If an internal modem is not included, go to point 38 to record the modems you've seen.

11. **Speakers Included:**   Yes ☐   No ☐
12. **Headphones:**   Yes ☐   No ☐
13. **Microphone:**   Yes ☐   No ☐
14. **Fax Capability:**   Yes ☐   No ☐

Numbers 11 through 14 are merely to note whether those features are included with the computer. The choice of machine is not necessarily made by the number of times you check "yes." It is based on which of the features matter to you.

15. **Type of Mouse:**_____ **Notes on Feel**:_____

If you are buying a desktop, it will come with a standard mouse. If you are buying a laptop, note which kind of mouse it comes with (trackball, touchpad, touchpoint). Jot down some notes on the feel of each. Remember, you can't be expected to master the mouse at this point, but you will have an impression of how it feels. Is the mouse positioned in a place that seems easy to access, or is your hand cramped while using it? Your mouse will be your constant companion when you're on the computer, so it must be comfortable to access and control. But generally speaking, control will come with practice.

16. **Notes on Keyboard:**_____

Note the feel of the keyboard. Do the keys feel mushy? Are they too resistant? Or are they just right?

17. **How Will It Fit in Your Workspace?** _____

Take notes on how you picture your computer system in your home.

SUPPORT

18. **Warranty:**_____

The length of the warranty will be in months. What parts fall under warranty?

19. **Extended Warranty:**_____ **Cost:**_____

It's more than likely that the computer store where you make your purchase will offer you an extended warranty. This is an agreement with the store or mail-order company, not the manufacturer. The agreement is valid only if the store is still operational for the duration of the extended warranty—a good reason to make sure you are shopping at a reputable store.

20. **Money-Back Guarantee:**_____

This may be an agreement with the manufacturer that you have a certain number of days to return the machine—kind of like the lemon law. Beware: some manufacturers will not exchange a computer even if it is defective. They may only offer to repair the machine. In that case you may want to engage your credit card company as an advocate for you. Or, before contacting the manufacturer, call the store you purchased it from and ask if it is willing to exchange the defective computer.

21. **Technical Support:**   Yes ☐   No ☐

This is crucial. You want to make sure that the store or mail-order company you purchase from has technical support. The last thing you want to have to do is pack up your computer and mail it to the manufacturer. It is irritating enough to have to bring it to the store for repairs. Ask specifically about telephone technical support. A lot of questions or problems can be answered by a telephone call to a technician.

You should be getting free support for the length of your warranty, whether you have a problem with your computer or you have a question about how to use the machine.

If the manufacturer, not the store, provides the technical support, ask your salesperson for the technical repair number of the manufacturers you are considering. When you are home, call the number and see how long it takes for you to speak to a technician. I've been on hold with some for over 20 minutes. This could be a deciding factor in determining which computer you purchase.

22. **On-Site Repair:**   Yes ☐   No ☐   **Cost:**_____

Can someone come to your home to repair your computer? How much will it cost if it is still under warranty? What if the warranty has expired?

23. **On-Site Installation:** Yes ☐   No ☐   Cost:_____

Can someone come to your house to install your system?

SOFTWARE

24. **Operating System:**_____
    Preinstalled Software:_____

Note the operating system in your computer (Windows 98, Windows 2000, Mac OS9, other) and any preinstalled application software.

25. **Additional Software:**_____Cost:_____
    Additional Software:_____Cost:_____

You may want to buy word-processing software or some other software based on your interest. We will talk about this choice in Chapter 8.

PRINTER

26. **Brand Name & Model:**_____

Include any numbers that follow the brand name—they will indicate the model.

27. **Cost:**_____

28. **Features:**   Color ☐   Black & White Only ☐
                     Fax ☐   Copy ☐   Scanner ☐

You will choose features based on your specific needs. A basic black-and-white printer may be all that you want. A color printer and scanner might be helpful if you decide to do something like a family newsletter or to make your own greeting cards. Color is also more fun if you're printing a web site. However, if you use a color printer, you have to purchase both a black ink cartridge and a color ink cartridge. Cartridges can be pricey.

29. **Paper Loading:**   Top ☐   Front ☐

It is important to note whether the printer is front or top loading so you can arrange your workspace accordingly.

30. Number of Pages Printed per Minute:_____

If you are anticipating a lot of printing, how quickly the printer works may be quite important to you.

31. Number of Pages Printed per Ink Cartridge:_____

This is an important issue. I have a student who was interested in having a small, portable printer. She was unpleasantly surprised when her ink cartridge ran out after less than 50 pages were printed and a replacement cartridge cost over $20.

32. Cost of Ink Cartridge Replacements:_____

33. Length of Warranty:_____

34. Extended Warranty:_____ **Cost:**_____

To repeat from point 19, it's more than likely that the computer store where you make your purchase will offer you an extended warranty. This is an agreement with the store, not the manufacturer. The agreement is valid only if the store is still operational for the duration of the extended warranty—a good reason to make sure you're shopping at a reputable store.

35. Money-Back Guarantee: _____

Full refund ☐   Store credit ☐   Other ☐

Again, this is an agreement with the manufacturer that you have a certain number of days to return the machine. Ask the store if you get a full refund or just a store credit.

36. Toll-Free Support: Yes ☐   No ☐

Remember, this is crucial. You want to make sure that the store you purchase from has technical support. You should be getting free support for the length of your warranty.

37. On-Site Repair: Yes ☐   No ☐   Cost:_____

Even with the printer, ask if someone can come to your home to repair it.

MODEM

(If a modem is not included with your computer, you will want to buy an external modem.)

38. Brand Name & Model:_____

Include any numbers that follow the brand name—they will indicate the model.

39. Speed:_____

The higher, the better. Go for nothing less than a 56K modem.

40. Cost:_____

41. Warranty:_____

Length of warranty in months.

42. Extended Warranty:_____**Cost:**_____

I am not sure this is really necessary for a modem, but let the salesperson explain why you might need it if the store is offering an extended warranty.

43. Money-Back Guarantee:_____

Again, this is an agreement with the manufacturer that you have a certain number of days to return the modem.

44. Toll-Free Support: Yes ☐ No ☐

Remember, this is crucial. You want to make sure that the store you purchase from has technical support. You should be getting free support for the length of your warranty.

45. Did you ask if all of the peripherals are compatible?

Make sure that all the parts you are buying are friendly with each other. Have your salesperson confirm this and note his or her name in case he or she is wrong.

Don't Buy Before You're Ready

Carol, one of my students, bought her computer but didn't want to get started for a couple of months. She ran the risk of not being able to utilize the free assistance the manufacturers offered at time of purchase.

It's a good idea to play with every aspect of your purchase soon after you get it home. Use the computer, your peripherals and your software.

Filling out this form may seem like a lot of work—perhaps more work than you've done buying anything else. This isn't just a way to have you make an educated purchase; it is also a way for you to learn about the machine you will be using. By the time you go through this process and get the computer home, you'll be much more knowledgeable than the average consumer. Your friends and family will be calling *you* for guidance!

Think of your first trip to the computer store as a dress rehearsal. What a relief to go in knowing that you don't have to make any big decisions or spend any money. You're just sightseeing. Bask in all the salesperson's attention and get as much information as you can, but feel no purchase pressure. Remember: This is only a test drive.

On Your Mark, Get Set, Go!

Okay. Let's make sure you have everything you need for your test drive.

• You have a copy of the Test-Drive Form from the back of the book. (You may even want to bring this book with you.)

• You have a sense of where you want to set up your computer and a note with any necessary measurements.

• You have thought about whether you want a desktop or a laptop and a Mac or a PC.

• You are equipped with magazine articles in which the computers and software that interest you have been noted.

• You have noted the recommendations of friends and family and any questions you may have.

• You have brought something to write with.

- You are in control. You may not completely understand what you're looking at, but that's fine. Make your salesperson prove his or her worth by helping you understand.

- You have chosen a nice place to have lunch. You deserve a lovely treat after all your hard work!

It's helpful to keep in mind that the performance pressure is on the salespeople, not you. When you get inside the store, the responsibility is on them to make you feel at home and to help you decide which computer best meets your needs. All you have to do is listen, take notes and ask questions (if you have any). Certainly it isn't necessary, but it wouldn't be a bad idea to bring along a computer-literate friend who can act as a translator if the high-tech jargon gets too thick.

And one last thing: *Enjoy yourself!* Remember, you don't have to make any decisions. Just look, listen and learn.

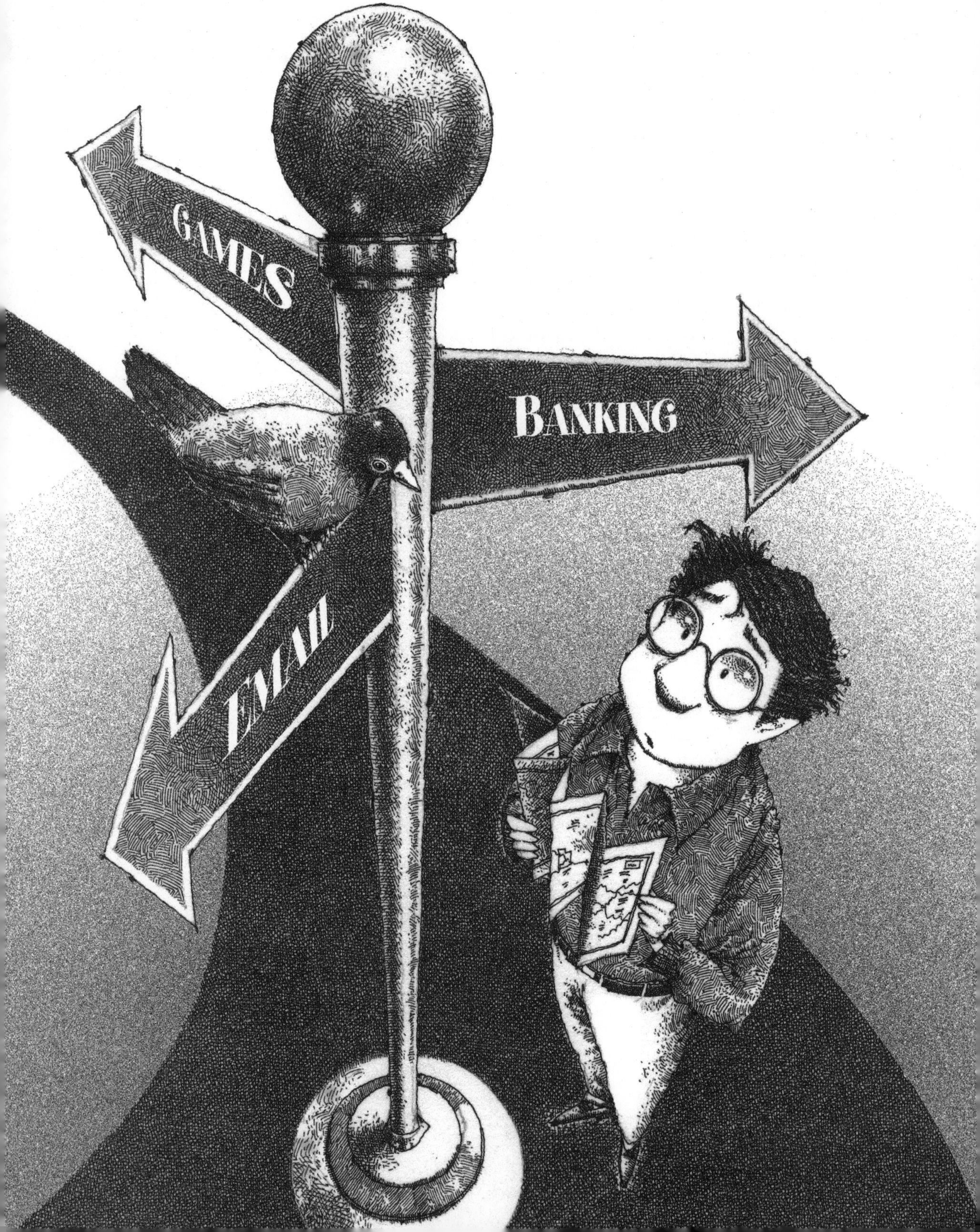
GAMES
BANKING
EMAIL

Choosing the Best Route
What software and Internet services fit you best

With the test drive behind you, we can now discuss your software options. However, before we talk further about software, review Chapter 3, which gives an explanation of software and how it is used.

All computers come with preinstalled operating software. The operating software functions as the road map and filing system of your computer. A computer *must* have operating software in order to function.

What Software Will Come with Your Computer?

Whether you buy a desktop or a laptop, a PC or a Mac, your computer will already have the operating software stored in its brain. Even though the operating software on a PC is different than on a Mac, both offer some features that let you get started right away. However, these are bare-bones features. You will probably want to investigate adding some application software to your computer at the time of purchase or shortly thereafter. (Remember: application software enables you to type a letter, design a web site, chart your family genealogy and much more.)

The manufacturer of your computer may have already added some application software to your computer. Just to toss some jargon your way, a salesperson might say, "Your computer already has software *loaded* on it." That means some application software has already been installed on your computer.

Each computer will be different in what may be pre-installed, but usually there will be word-processing software (Microsoft Word, WordPerfect, or Claris), sometimes financial management software (such as Quicken) and often some fun stuff (simulated golf, solitaire, etc.). This preinstalled application software is also referred to as "bundled software."

Buyer Beware

When a store offers to sell you a computer "bundled" with software, it may sound convenient, but it does have a downside. When you do not buy the software outright—by that I mean you actually own the installation disk—you may have trouble getting technical assistance if you need it. Each set of installation disks has a serial or registration number. With this number the manufacturer confirms that you have purchased the software and will then offer you technical assistance. This is the manufacturers' way to protect themselves against people who have "pirated" software (not bought, but borrowed and installed). Another downside of bundled software: You won't get the operation manuals.

An example is a student of mine who bought a Toshiba laptop that had been bundled with Microsoft Word (application software for word processing). When she had a problem with the software, she called Microsoft for help, but because she didn't have the installation disks, they said that they were not authorized to help her. When she called Toshiba, she was told that they were not equipped to assist her with Microsoft Word software, but if she had a question about her Toshiba computer they would be happy to help. Neither Toshiba nor Microsoft was at fault. She shouldn't have had her word-processing software bundled onto her

> **"** *My son bought me software so that I could create a family tree and track our genealogy. It is marvelous. Once I'm done I'll be able to give copies to all the kids.* **"**
> —Martina

machine. It isn't illegal for the stores to bundle software, but it may prove unwise for you in the long run.

It is tempting when someone offers to bundle software with your computer purchase. However, I strongly advise that you consider making the extra investment of buying the software to have the security of technical assistance and the manual, in case you need either. Alternatively, you can check with your salesperson to see if the store will provide technical support for the bundled software. If they will, then you might want to consider it.

What If You Want to Buy Additional Software?

In addition to what your computer will already have installed in it, you may want to purchase some application software. Whatever application software you may be interested in, there are some things you should check out before you make a purchase.

Compatibility: You *must* make sure that the software is compatible with your computer. On the outside of the software box, it will indicate which operating system it is friendly with (Mac OS9, Windows 98, Windows 2000, etc.). Make sure your operating system is listed. The manufacturer should also post how much space, speed and RAM it needs to operate properly. (When you buy your computer, you'll record the size of your hard drive and the speed of your CPU. Always have it handy when you go shopping for software.)

A Reminder of Different Kinds of Application Software

Word Processing—lets you type letters, recipes, a novel
Financial Management—helps you track accounts, print checks, pay bills
Organizational—helps you maintain a calendar, address book, home inventory
Communication—enables you to travel the Internet, send faxes and e-mail
Educational—offers you typing instruction, languages, reference materials
Graphics—lets you create pictures, design cards, invitations
Entertainment—offers lots of games, games, games

The Lowdown on Word-Processing Software

The two front-runners for word-processing software are Microsoft Word and WordPerfect. The differences between these two products are not huge, and the choice is really subjective. Before choosing the word-processing software that is best for you, it is a good idea to check it out on someone else's computer. You might be able to try it out at the store, but that is not a common practice.

There is a danger in buying a lesser-known software. You will get very used to how your word-processing software operates. If, over time, the company that manufactured your software goes out of business, you are stuck with that version of software. And as new technology develops, you won't be able to upgrade to a newer version.

Popularity: It's valuable to find out what the top-selling software is. It still may not be the right choice for you, but there is a reason why it is so popular. Ask your salesperson why a particular software dominates the market.

Pull Out Those Magazines: The same magazines that listed the top ten computers to buy will also list the top ten software products.

Friends and Family: Again, if your friends or family have computers, ask which software they're using and why. Have they been happy with it? Can they do a little show-and-tell for you? Keep in mind that people are very loyal to their choice of software. This sense of loyalty should not convince you; the performance of the software should.

Salespeople: Ask them about software products and have them give you a demonstration. They really do have your best interests in mind. Also ask if they can install it for you and what that will cost. Installing software isn't difficult to do on your own, but if you buy it at the same time you buy your computer, the store may install it for you as a courtesy.

Help!: Find out if the software manufacturer offers technical support. Is it free? For how long is it free? Some software manufacturers offer free support for the first 90 days after purchase. If that is the case, it's a good idea to play with the software right away to get out any bugs and take advantage of the free help.

Cost: Some software is surprisingly expensive. If it seems out of your price range, ask your salesperson if he or she can recommend something similar without all the bells and whistles. The same manufacturer that designed the expensive software may offer a pared-down version for substantially less.

Online Services Software

The modem is the hardware that allows you to connect to the Internet, but you'll also need specific software. There are many companies that supply software to connect your computer, via the modem, to the outside world. These companies are called online services and they provide you with access to e-mail and the Internet. To be sure there is no misunderstanding—you *must* have an online service in order to access the Internet or send e-mail.

Your computer manufacturer (for both Mac and PC) may have included application software for several online services preinstalled on your hard drive. Some of the more popular companies may be familiar to you—America Online, Microsoft Network, Earthlink and CompuServe, to name a few.

When the time comes, you will sign on to one of these providers by using a credit card, which will be automatically charged each month for your subscription to their service. Right now the average cost of unlimited use is $20 a month. This allows you to send and receive e-mail and surf the net 24 hours a day, 7 days a week.

If the computer you're thinking of buying does not have online services preinstalled on the hard drive, call any of the services in the back of the book and they will be more than happy to send you the software so you can install their program. The software for online services is free because they make their money from the monthly usage charges.

If you are using a direct service line (DSL) or a cable company is providing your Internet connection, they will give you the necessary software. A cable connection is much faster than using the phone line, but it comes with a higher price tag.

How Will I Know Which Online Service to Choose?

This decision is subjective. There is no online service that is "the best." Again, signing on to a service that your friends and family use is always smart in case you need some help.

Call the online service provider you are considering to be sure they offer a local access number in your area. Otherwise, you may incur long-distance charges on your phone bill—and those can add up.

Microsoft Network's (MSN) Home Page.

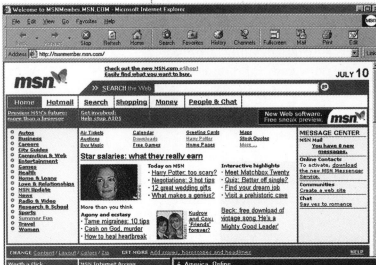

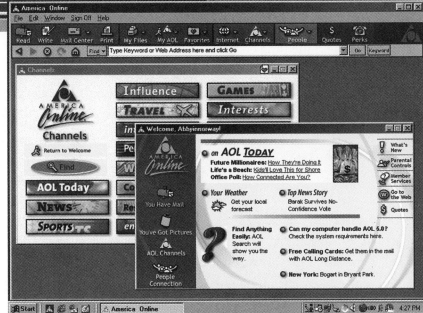

America Online's (AOL) Home Page.

With any of these services it's a good idea to call their technical support number and see how long you are kept on hold. Inevitably you will need to call them with a question,

Earthlink's Home Page.

and if they are impossible to reach, that could be a factor in your decision-making process. Remember, you're not married to whichever service you start with. Lots of them offer at least 30-day or 30-hour trial periods for free. Take advantage of these promotional offers and see which one appeals to you.

Shown here are the "home pages" of a few different online services. A Home Page is a combination of the cover of a book and its index and will be the first thing you see every time you go online. From the Home Page you can access all the features of the service, including e-mail and the Internet. Use the Home Pages shown here as another way of judging which online service you might prefer. If a page shown here appears too messy or confusing, it may not be the right service for you. However, don't feel that you need to understand everything you see. When the time comes to explore the Internet, all will become clear.

It is very important that you remember to cancel your trial subscription if you no longer want the online service. Even though the company won't bill you for the trial period, they will have asked for your credit card information to start the account. If you forget to cancel the account, they will start billing your credit card when the trial period is over and continue to do so until you cancel your subscription.

Local Online Services

My mother uses a local online service. Southern New England Telephone (SNET) offered her a good deal, and she's been very happy with it. Her monthly subscription charges go on her phone bill rather than on her credit card. You may want to call your local phone company to see what they have to offer.

For Now, Keep it Simple

The only application software decision that you need to make soon is which online service you want to use. All other software can be purchased over time. The decision about your online service isn't such a big deal because that application software will be free and you can change your mind and use a different service at any time.

Let the Shopping Begin

9 Shop Till You Drop
Old vs. new, extended warranties, store vs. mail order and what questions to ask

Now that you're armed with the experience of your test drive and have thought through your application software choices, let's address a few more options before you make your big purchase. There are some decisions that involve a little gambling, but with careful thought and consideration you'll never have to say, "I can't believe I took such a chance." We'll go over all the bets, sure and otherwise, and I'll tell you what the odds favor. I promise, if you do your homework, you'll love your computer choice.

Hand-me-downs

There are always people looking to sell their used computers to finance the purchase of the newest machine on the market. Because technology evolves so quickly, a computer can begin to look like a dinosaur in just a couple of years. However, that's really an issue only for people who use all the features on their computer to the fullest. For most of us, that's not the case.

People sell perfectly good used machines not because anything is wrong with them but because they want

Missing Parts

When you buy used equipment, you must be very sure that all the parts end up in your hands. There are a lot of cables that run from one piece of equipment to another, so make a deal with the seller to set up the computer for you. This way you can make sure everything you need is there and that it all works. You must also be sure to get any manuals that came with the equipment and any installation disks for the software on the computer.

something more. Perhaps they want more speed, more hard drive space or some new feature their old machine doesn't have. Their old machine may be just right for you. That said, be cautious about whom you purchase used equipment from. You don't want to buy someone else's headache. Never buy a used computer without knowing its history.

It is probably safest to buy only from a friend or family member. If it is one of your kids who wants to buy a new computer and sell the old one, forge ahead! If your local high school is looking to replace their computers, you might get a great deal and personal technical support. Ask if one of the students can set it up for you and give you a demonstration. But if it's someone you don't know who is advertising in the newspaper, think twice. What is your recourse if it breaks down? Probably none. The odds are not in your favor if you buy a computer from a stranger.

Guidelines to Buying Used Equipment

Before you opt to buy a used computer, consider the following:

1. Is the CPU at least 266MHz? *Translation: The CPU, as we have discussed, is what guides everything on your computer. The speed of it should be no less than 266MHz (megahertz). Anything slower will hinder your use of the Internet, and you might have problems adding software in the future.*

2. Does it have at least 64MB of RAM? *Translation: The RAM is the memory that is used when the computer is on. In order to open web sites on the Internet and send e-mail, you will need at least 64MB of RAM.*

3. If it is a PC, does it have Windows 95? *Translation: Windows 95 is an operating system to help organize your files and documents. You need to have at least Windows 95 in order to buy any software; Windows 98 is even better.*

4. Is the hard drive at least 1GB? *Translation: The hard drive is where everything on your computer is stored. 1GB = 1 gigabyte. That is the minimum space you should have.*

Any less space than that and you'll have problems adding software.

5. Is the modem at least 56KB? *Translation: Modems run at a particular speed, measured in kilobytes (not unlike megabytes or gigabytes, discussed earlier). A modem with less than 56KB is too slow.*

6. Is the screen in full color? *Although I haven't seen one in a while, there are old screens that are just shades of gray or amber. Don't let someone pawn one of those off on you. It'll take most of the fun out of using the computer if you can't see the images in their full glory.*

7. If you are looking at used printers, have the seller print a page from the printer for you. Do you like the quality of the print? How long did it take to print a page? If it's a black-and-white printer, has your heart been set on getting one that can print in color? *Make sure they include all the cables and software for the printer. There should be a cord that goes from the printer to the computer and one that goes from the printer to the electrical outlet. Remember your workspace—does the printer fit where you want to put it?*

8. How much does it cost? *Any used computer approaching $500 is too much. You can buy a new desktop that fits the criteria described starting at about $600. And a new computer will come with some type of warranty and technical support. A used computer bought for the same price without that support would be a foolish purchase. Any used printer for $75 or more is too much. You can buy a new color inkjet printer starting at around $140.*

> **"**I figured I had nothing to lose if I bought a cheap used computer. I wasn't even sure I was going to like it. I did the math and decided it was worth it, even if I replaced it a year later with something better.**"**
> —Harvey

9. Can it be upgraded? *Ask what the maximum CPU, hard drive and RAM capacities are. If the previous owner has upgraded the computer to its highest capacity—brought the CPU, hard drive and RAM to the maximum—you might outgrow the machine, and you won't have the option to beef it up.*

10. Trust your instincts. *If something smells fishy with the used machine, say, "Thanks, but no thanks," and walk away. No obligation. If it smells sweet, buy it and enjoy.*

Upgrading . . . Infuriating

It all sounds fine and dandy that an older computer can be upgraded, but it isn't that simple. Once someone opens up the machine to make an adjustment, you run the risk of something being damaged. The inside of a computer is a very fragile thing, and the components there have a relationship to one another that should be left alone if at all possible. On more than one occasion I've had students whose upgrades turned into low-grade headaches. Tread carefully if someone says that the machine just needs an upgrade to meet your specifications. Upgrading the computer will also entail your taking the machine to a store for the work to be done.

Something else to keep in mind: When you upgrade a laptop, it can cost more than upgrading a desktop computer. Some manufacturers don't design their laptops to be compatible with other manufacturers' hardware. For example, if you want to increase the RAM in your laptop, you might only be able to buy your laptop manufacturer's upgrade at their price. It's the old monopoly game. This policy is less common with desktop models.

If New Is the Only Thing for You

I just gave you the minimums that you should accept for a used computer. If you're buying a new computer, use the following criteria as your *minimums,* but feel free to surpass them. (Once your computer purchase is made, you won't have to think about all this technical mumbo jumbo.)

☞ **CPU**—*500MHz*

☞ **Hard Drive**—*6GB to 10GB*

☞ **RAM**—*128MB*

☞ **Modem**—*56KB*

☞ **CD-ROM Drive**

☞ **PC Operating System**—*Windows 2000*

☞ **Mac Operating System**—*8.0*

One of the great advantages when you buy a new computer is the warranty and technical service offered. Most new machines will have a limited warranty of 30, 60, or 90 days offered by the manufacturer.

Are Extended Warranties Warranted?

An extended warranty will probably be from the store where you made your purchase, not the manufacturer. Double-check with your salesperson whether a warranty is from the store or from the manufacturer. Regardless of who offers the warranty, make sure you understand the terms. There is no advantage to the warranty being from either the store or the manufacturer. You just want to be sure that whoever offers the warranty is going to stay in business for the time that you have the computer.

Ask friends and family if they know of a computer whiz who makes house calls. My mother was given a great recommendation from the computer class at her local senior center. She got the job done at home and paid a lot less than she would have at a technical service department.

Ask questions: How long has the store been in existence? Is it part of a chain? What is their reputation? When I bought my television, I purchased an extended warranty. In less than six months, the store I bought it from went out of business. At this point the manufacturer had the option of honoring my warranty. They chose not to. Surprise, surprise. Lucky for me, I've never had any problems with the set.

Once you've determined that the store is reputable, be sure to ask your salesperson what the extended warranty covers and what it costs. If it sounds good, I advise you to buy it. When things go wrong with a computer, it can be mighty expensive to repair. The episode I mentioned in Chapter 5, with my spilling milk on my laptop, could have set me back several hundred dollars, but thankfully, I was still under warranty.

Some extended warranties are based on the price range of your total purchase. Others are based on the price of individual items. Example: One store may offer a certain priced extended warranty for purchases, say, from $1,500 to $2,000 (combining the cost of your computer and printer). Another store may require that you purchase separate warranties for each item. You will save money by purchasing a single extended warranty based on the total cost of your computer and printer or any other peripherals if the store allows that. Some salespeople may not tell you this is their store policy and will instead offer you two separate warranties. Be sure to investigate.

Also ask if the preinstalled application software (probably something like Microsoft Word and Quicken) is covered under the extended warranty. Do you remember when I warned you about having software "bundled" at the time of purchase on p. 68 in Chapter 8? Some stores offer to give you support for the bundled software under their warranty. If this is the case, the warnings I gave earlier can be ignored.

The last thing you need to check out is where any repair work will be done. Can they come to your house? What is the charge for an on-site visit? An on-site visit is obviously the most convenient choice, but it may also be the most expensive. If it's too expensive, do you have to bring the machine to the location where you bought it? Does it need to be mailed somewhere else to be repaired? Mail-in repair may not suit you. It probably means that you need to keep the original boxes for packing so that you can schlep it from your house to the post office—and you'll be without the machine longer because of mailing time. I think it is a huge inconvenience, but I live in Manhattan and would have to battle my way on the subway from my house to a post office lugging the monstrosity. Ugh.

Mail Order

Now that you've gone for a test drive and have a feel for several different computers, you can think about the pros and cons of buying your machine by mail order. As with purchasing a computer in a store, buying mail order without test driving is definitely not recommended.

Mail order is not limited to finding what you need in a catalog, picking up a phone and placing your order. If someone you know is already on the Internet, have him or her help you visit the manufacturer's web site so that you can view the computers, configure your ideal machine and order it on the spot. Delivery is usually a week to ten days.

Mail order can be a very convenient way to shop, but there is a downside. Most of the mail-order computer manufacturers do not offer on-site repair unless you buy one of their more expensive machines or pay extra for the service. If you don't want to make that kind of investment, your options are to hire someone to come to your home or to try to correct the problem yourself over the phone with a support technician. If you can't fix it with one of those options, you'll have to send the machine to the manufacturer . . . and you know what that entails. For me, that's a real turn-off.

Reputation Counts

You want to pick a mail-order company and a computer manufacturer with a solid reputation. There's a list of computer mail-order catalogs in the back of this book. Dell, Compaq and Gateway are the first that come to mind as mail-order manufacturers with great reputations. Always pay with a credit card so you have recourse if the computer ends up being a lemon.

Buyer's Remorse

If, after you have bought your computer, you either change your mind or the computer isn't all it's cracked up to be, you may not be able to return it. Macintosh has a no-return policy even if the computer is defective. They will repair the machine but not replace it. Other manufacturers are beginning to follow suit. I find this appalling. The only way to get around returning a defective machine is to *not* report the problem to the manufacturer, but instead call the store that you bought it from. The store may be willing to exchange the computer if you haven't registered it with the manufacturer. Ask your salesperson for the store's return policy. If the computer has any bugs, you will find them out immediately. That's why it is so important to use the machine right away.

If you are using a laptop and the computer is plugged into a surge protector, the surge protector needs to remain on for the battery to be able to charge.

Additional Accessories

There are a few small items that you should purchase when you buy a used or new computer. All are relatively inexpensive, and it will be easier to get them at the same time you make your "big" purchase.

Surge Protector

The electrical cords for your computer and any peripherals should be plugged into a surge protector. It maintains a constant flow of power to whatever is plugged in to it, thereby protecting your equipment from irregular power surges. A change in the flow of electrical power can cause damage to your computer.

Buy a surge protector that has a cord long enough to reach an outlet. If your outlet is only a two-hole outlet, you can purchase an adapter for the surge protector at any hardware store for about a dollar. The important thing to remember with a three-prong adapter is that it needs to be properly grounded. This isn't hard to do—someone at the hardware store can talk you through it.

Wrist Rest

A wrist rest allows your wrist to maintain an unbroken line from your elbow to fingertips when working on the keyboard. This keeps you from straining your wrist and can help prevent discomfort and, more specifically, carpal tunnel syndrome, a wrist injury that results from inflammation of the tendons. It is common among tennis players, pianists and computer users.

Mouse Pad

A mouse pad helps you have better control of the mouse. It is a smooth rubber pad similar in dimension to a face cloth and about a quarter-inch thick. You will manipulate the mouse by sliding it on top of the mouse pad. It is very difficult to control a mouse without a pad.

Now What?

Well, it's finally time to go back to the store for your purchase, get on the phone or have someone access a web site where you can buy a computer. For this shopping trip you need many of the same things that you used for the test drive:

- A blank piece of paper and something to write with
- The measurements of your workspace
- A list of what your computer must have to suit your needs

- Your filled-in Test-Drive Form and your marked magazine articles. (*If you have already decided on the computer you want to buy, you may not need to bring these with you.*)

- A blank Test-Drive Form. *Have your salesperson fill this in with the details of your new computer. If you are ordering over the phone, you can still go over the form with your salesperson. If you are ordering over the Internet, the web site should provide you with all the necessary information to fill out the form.*

- Means to pay for your purchase. *Preferably a credit card and proper photo identification.*

- If you are buying your computer at a store, bring a friend. *If for no better reason than to help you carry things to the car.*

- Butterflies in your stomach. *It's only natural when you're about to embark upon a new adventure.*

Get the Most Out of Your Salesperson

Never let a salesperson smooth-talk you into something you feel is excessive or that you're not comfortable with. You always have the prerogative to go home and think it over or say "no" on the spot. There is no need to be impulsive. Take all the time you need to make your decision and rest assured that you are well informed. The person selling you the computer needs you more than you need him or her.

Here are some suggestions on how to take control of your shopping experience and have the salesperson do the best for you.

Set the scene. Give salespeople as much information as you can. If they start to lead you around the store before you've explained exactly what you want, halt the process. Just stop in your tracks and say, "Let's first talk about what I

These suggestions for getting the most out of your salesperson hold true if you're purchasing by telephone as well. Let the salesperson know you have all the time in the world to make the right decision.

know I want and some questions I have." In the middle of a crazy day, people can run on automatic—bring them back to a human level. I've seen salespeople relax when given a chance to deviate from their "routine speech." Look them in the eye and let them see you as an individual who needs their expert guidance.

Be honest. Let them know that you've done research. You can even show them your notes. If you're uneasy with something, tell them. Perhaps you're concerned about how to connect the cords to the ports at the back of the computer when you get home. Upon hearing this, your sympathetic salesperson might offer to send someone over to help you. Or might not. Instead, the salesperson may give you an in-store demonstration. Feel free to ask for such a demonstration. A refusal would be the worst that can happen, and may be an indication you should take your business elsewhere.

Slow the process down. Computer salespeople often miss the mark because they assume that we're all comfortable with computers and understand the jargon that goes along with them. I've been working with computers for over ten years and still find myself asking salespeople to slow down and explain themselves in plain English.

If, as you tell your salesperson what you need, he or she looks ready to start a 20-yard dash, state that you're not in any rush. "If you can't give me the time I need, I'd be happy to speak with someone else." I know it sounds a bit harsh, but the salesperson is probably used to people who want to come in, make their purchase and get out. Asking the salesperson to slow down will come as a surprise, but it may be a welcome one—it gives him or her a chance to relax and not "work" so hard.

If You Still Aren't Sure

If after all your research you still haven't decided which computer you want, ask the salesperson to show you the top

> **❝** *I went back to the computer store with more questions and a friend. We gave the salesman a run for his money. . . I don't think he expected us to know as much as we did. It all ended happily—we went home with computers and he made two big sales.* **❞**
> —Phyllis

Review What You're Interested in Buying

Before you set foot into your local computer store to buy a machine, decide on the following:

- *Size of your available workspace* (Review Chapter 5)
- *Laptop vs. desktop* (Review Chapter 4)
- *Mac vs. PC* (Review Chapter 6)

Here are a few other things that you should have done by now:

- *Checked out computers of friends and family*
- *Researched computer magazines for their recommendations*
- *Gone for a test-drive*
- *Reviewed your filled-in Test-Drive Form*

two computers that interest you. Then ask to see the models just higher and lower in price to give you a better feel for what's right for you. Don't deviate from your budget, but do make sure you're buying a computer that meets all your needs.

Return Policy

What is the store's return policy? There may be a certain number of days that you can return your computer for no better reason than you've changed your mind or you don't like the color. However, if you want to take advantage of this, you'd better get the new machine up and running in that amount of time. No procrastinating on this or you will be in the soup! Be delicate with the packaging. Some stores won't accept returns if the package is damaged.

Keeping Track of Things

Be sure to ask your salesperson for a couple of business cards. If you have any questions down the road, his or her telephone number will be at your fingertips. Also ask the salesperson to fill in the blank Test-Drive Form. This will prove a helpful record of the computer and peripherals you have bought.

At this point, the success of your shopping trip is not based on luck. You have all the information that you need to make a wise computer purchase. I wasn't as well informed when I bought my first computer, and it served me well for seven years. Go to your computer store confident that you know more about computers than the average customer. When you get home with your new machine and you want to set it up, I will be waiting for you in Chapter 10.

Baby's First Day Home

10

Counting Fingers and Toes
Taking your new computer out of the box and connecting all the parts

You are now in all likelihood the proud owner of a new computer. Congratulations! Give yourself a pat on the back from me.

From this point forward, we'll be doing hands-on work with your computer. Don't worry, you don't have to be a rocket scientist. You can read through the chapter if you want, but then come back to this page and follow the instructions step by step. Illustrated setup instructions will also be included with your new computer. (Be forewarned—these may be harder to follow than your tax return.) The instructions below will help simplify the process. Read them along with the instructions that come with your computer.

Set the Scene

There are three things that you must do before you even open your computer boxes.

First, find a large (at least 8″ × 12″) mailing envelope or a gallon self-sealing plastic bag that can be closed securely. Label it "Computer Information." Put all your sales receipts

66 *Some people may feel comfortable setting up their own computer, but I would rather spend the money to have someone come and do it for me.*99
—Kathy

and any other paperwork from the computer store into the envelope or bag. If your salesperson filled out the Test-Drive Form when you made your purchase, you can skip the steps below. If you don't have a filled-out computer Test-Drive Form, take a clean piece of paper and write down the following information on it:

- The date of purchase.

- The store where you made your purchase, as well as the phone number and name of your salesperson (or staple the salesperson's card to the piece of paper).

- Look on the outside of your computer's packing box. It will probably have a description of your computer. If it does, copy down the brand name of your computer and any numbers or letters that follow—this indicates the model. Most likely the speed of your CPU, size of your hard drive and speed of your RAM will also appear on the outside of the box. Note these as well. Next, write down the speed of your modem. Last but not least, write down any peripherals you bought—printer, scanner, modem (include brand and model). If this information isn't on the packing boxes, you can get the details when you set up the computer.

- Note the length of the warranty and extended warranty, if you purchased one.

Put all this documentation inside your "Computer Information" packet.

The **second** thing you have to do is make space. Don't try to set up the computer in an area where there's a lot of clutter. It not only makes for a pleasant work environment when there is plenty of space, but the computer also needs proper ventilation. Look at the workspace that you want to use for the computer, and move everything that's in your way to the other end of the room. You can move things back eventually, but it's much easier to keep track of what you're doing (and much less frustrating) if you have plenty of room to work in. If you are unsure of your workspace, go back to Chapter 5 for a quick review of some factors to consider in choosing one.

Third, have a pair of scissors, box of rubber bands, wastebasket, roll of masking tape and small box or an available section of a bookshelf at the ready.

Before you connect all the parts, feel free to ask a computer-owning friend or family member to help you. This is not a test of your ability to last four days in the forest alone. If someone in the know is willing to set up your computer, for goodness' sake let them do it. Maybe you've even convinced someone from the computer store—or a high-school student—to help. Just be sure that you pay attention to what's done. Take notes if you want to. There may come a time when you'll move the computer, and it will be helpful to understand how it's all connected.

❝I wanted to put it together myself. I figured it was the best way to get to know the machine. I did it very slowly.❞
—Ralph

The Moment We've Been Waiting For

If you've bought a laptop or iMac, the unpacking stage is quite simple. There will only be your computer, an electrical cord and a few incidental items to unpack. However, if you've bought a desktop, there will be several large items— a monitor, the computer case, the keyboard and several cords to connect everything.

1. Use scissors to cut open the box. *Be gentle.* Not only is your investment inside, but if you do have buyer's remorse, you'll have to return the computer in its original package. Try not to destroy the box or the big pieces of packing materials. My sister saves all her equipment boxes. She has moved several times, and it gives her great comfort to have

The main components of your desktop computer are the computer case, monitor, keyboard and mouse.

Compatibility

It is very important that whatever extras you buy for your computer are compatible with your system. If you get home and the salesclerk was wrong and the parts are not compatible, take them back to the store!

her computer happily secure in its original boxes—safe from the dangers of burly, careless movers.

2. If you've bought a desktop, be aware that the computer case and the monitor can be quite heavy and unwieldy. It is a good idea to gently set the box on its side and drag the piece of equipment out of the box along the floor. If you think it's too heavy for you, do *not* try to take it out of the box yourself. You don't want to hurt yourself or damage the computer. If it all seems manageable, gently remove the computer parts from their boxes and set them carefully on the floor.

3. Each packing box will also contain the proper cords. As an extra precaution, you can stop now and label each cord with masking tape. Example: Mark "Monitor cord to outlet" on the end that plugs into the wall and "Monitor cord to computer case" on the other end. "Keyboard cord to computer case," and so on. That way, if you move the computer, there'll be no confusion about which cord goes to which part.

4. Until all the parts are unveiled, it's safest to have them where they can't be knocked over. The instructional books, warranties, installation disks and small parts included with your computer should be placed by the part they came with and kept together with a rubber band. Eventually all these things will be stored in the box that you set aside or on the available space on your bookshelf. If there is anything really tiny that might get lost, put it in your "Computer Information" envelope.

5. On each piece of equipment (whether it is a laptop or a desktop) there is a serial number (usually on the back or bottom). Take the piece of paper with all your computer information on it and jot down these serial numbers. Be clear about which serial number goes with which item. It's *much easier* to record these numbers now than after the computer has been set up. This is also the time to record the brand and model if it wasn't on the box.

Once all the parts of your computer are out of the box, sit down. Take a few minutes and just look at everything. Does it all look familiar to you?

It's very important that you don't misplace any of the floppy disks or CD-ROMs that came with your equipment. These are the installation disks for the operating software and are used as backup if your computer breaks down. It is unusual, but there is always the chance that your computer might have a major failure and lose everything stored in its memory. If for some reason the software (either operating or application) is affected, you will use these disks to reinstall.

Also set aside any registration cards that came with your equipment. They should be filled out and sent in after you're sure everything is in working order. The piece of paper where you recorded all the serial numbers will be your resource to complete the registration cards.

Take time to look over the written material that came with your computer, including the illustrated brochure on how to set everything up. No matter how tempting it is to forge ahead and hook everything up, don't. It is very important that you follow the instructions that the manufacturer has given, along with the steps below. Once a mistake has been made and something is hooked up improperly, it is a bear to backtrack and make a correction.

Examine the Ports

Before you plug anything in, get acquainted with the ports at the back of your computer. Notice that the cords and ports are designed as pairs; the number of holes in one port corresponds to the number of prongs on one of the cords. If, when you begin plugging things in, you feel any resistance, remove the cord and confirm that it matches the port.

The ports at the back of the computer case are where the cords plug in.

Be aware that the prongs on the cords are very delicate. If you bend one of the prongs, gently, very gently, urge it back to its original position.

Putting It All Together

If you have chosen a laptop or the iMac, setup is very simple: set the computer on your desk and plug the electrical cord into the back of the computer. *Do not* plug it into the wall yet.

If you have a desktop, the procedure for attaching all the parts of the computer is the same, whether you have purchased a Mac or a PC. As you follow these directions, you might also want to refer to the manufacturer's instructions along the way.

1. Gently and carefully pick up the **computer case** and place it where you want it. (Remember, don't place the computer case directly on carpeting, as it may generate static electricity that can harm the unit.) Most likely, the computer case will be on top of your desk, unless you have a tower case, which will probably go on the floor next to or under your desk. Don't forget you're going to want the computer case where you can easily reach it. Position it so that the ports at the back are still within reach. You will swing it into its final position once everything is plugged in. Attach the electrical cord to the back of the computer case, but *do not* plug it into the wall outlet yet.

2. The **monitor** should be placed either on top of your desk or on top of the computer case on your desk. The monitor is very fragile and very heavy. If you can't manage it, leave it where it is and ask someone to help you. Attach the cord that connects the monitor to the computer case.

Then take the electrical cord for the monitor and plug it into the back of the monitor. *Do not* plug it into the outlet yet.

3. The **keyboard** should be placed on your desk or pull-out shelf and plugged into the appropriate port on the computer case.

4. Set the **mouse** to the right of the keyboard and plug it in. Usually the mouse plugs into the computer case. If it doesn't, it will plug into the keyboard or sometimes even the monitor. Refer to the setup page in the instruction book that came with your computer to be sure. If you have a mouse pad, place it under the mouse.

5. If the **modem** is not built into your machine, connect the modem according to its instruction sheet. The computer should have come with a phone cord for your modem. Plug this phone cord into the hole that looks like a phone jack on the modem. Plug the other end of the phone cord into the phone jack on your wall. If the phone cord isn't long enough to reach the jack, you may have to buy a longer one.

6. If you have bought a **printer,** a **scanner** or any other peripheral, place it where you want it to be. Plug in the cord that goes from the printer or scanner to the computer case. Sometimes the end that plugs into the printer or scanner has some wire hinges; snap those into place. The end that connects to the computer case will probably have screws on either side. Once the cord is plugged in, turn the screws just enough to ensure that the cord doesn't dislodge. Plug the electrical cord into the printer or scanner, but *do not* plug it into the wall.

Before you plug anything into the electrical outlet, let's review what we have done so far.

• The monitor, keyboard, printer and any other peripherals are plugged into the back of your computer case.

• The mouse is plugged into either the computer case, monitor or keyboard.

• The monitor, computer case, printer and/or scanner

Attention, Southpaws

The mouse can also be positioned to the left of your keyboard. However, if you bought a PC, the function of the mouse buttons will be reversed. We're going to rectify that in Chapter 12. You might want to leave the mouse on the right side of the computer until then. If you bought a Mac, you can set the mouse on either side of the keyboard.

I have several students who write with their left hand but manipulate the mouse with their right. Try it both ways to see which you prefer.

The mouse is positioned with the "tail" pointing away from you.

also have cords that will eventually plug into an electrical source.

• The phone cord is plugged into your modem and the phone jack.

Sit back and view your creation. The last step is to plug it all into your electrical source. Take a break now and do something else, or if you're up to it, you can take the next big step.

Oops— Something's Missing

Are you missing a cord? Before you call the store, make sure that you've looked in all your boxes and on the floor where you unpacked everything. It is unusual for a cord not to be packed with the equipment, but it isn't impossible. Once you're sure that the cord isn't hiding somewhere, inform your salesperson that you are missing a cord. It's a drag, but you will probably have to go back to the store to pick it up.

Plug It In, Plug It In

Take the surge protector and position it near all the power cords. *Do not* plug it into the wall yet. Plug the monitor, computer case, printer and any other peripherals into the surge protector. Finally—*plug the surge protector into the wall outlet!* There may be an indicator light on the surge protector to let you know that it is connected. If that light is not lit, there should be an on/off switch on the surge protector; flip the switch and the light should go on.

At this point all the parts of the computer are attached and they are plugged into a power source. In the next chapter you will turn the computer on and begin to learn what an incredible resource it really is. Congratulations!

Labeling the cords that connect the parts of the computer proves helpful if you ever have to move the computer.

A Few Words on Safety

In the next chapter, we're going to begin working on the computer. For your safety and good health keep the following ergonomic guidelines in mind:

1. Your knees, hips and elbows should be at 90-degree angles.
2. There should be an unbroken line from your elbows to your fingertips—no breaking at the wrists.
3. Your hand should be relaxed when using the keyboard and the mouse—no claws or strain.
4. Be very aware of your posture—it is easy to "sink into" the machine over time.
5. The monitor should be an arm's length away. This may require a special prescription if you wear glasses.
6. *Take a break!* Do not sit at the computer for more than 40 minutes without taking a break to stretch and rest your eyes.

For your computer's health and well-being keep the computer away from:

1. Extreme heat or cold
2. Liquids of any kind
3. Dirt, dust and animal hair
4. Magnets
5. High-pile carpeting

11

Shaking Hands
Meet your computer and mouse

The time has come to turn on your new arrival. It may seem unnecessary to have part of a chapter devoted to turning on the computer, but it is a bit involved and can cause some confusion. You're about to embark on a wonderful new adventure and I will be by your side through the whole process. However, feel free to have a friend or family member also join you during any part of this journey.

The Ground Rules

My experience with students is that most people ask too much of themselves during the learning process. If I'm teaching you how to use the computer, you have to play by my rules.

- Do *not* try to memorize what we do. Eventually it will become second nature. Just follow the instructions—time and repetition will take care of the rest.
- Do *not* get hung up on understanding everything. I don't understand exactly how the computer works, but I follow the formula of how to make it work.
- Trying can be trying. If you've hit your saturation point or you're frustrated, simply stop. Put down the book. Leave the computer as it is and go do something else. If you

66 For three months I was afraid to turn my computer on. I would sit facing the ominous black screen and feel increasingly defeated. How times have changed—I just set up a friend's computer without a glitch!99
—Mark

don't return to the computer for an hour or a few days, it doesn't matter. The computer isn't going anywhere. Eventually your computer is where you'll go for fun, but at the beginning it can seem more like work.

Turning It On

There is no hard-and-fast rule about which parts of the computer should be turned on in what order, but I always turn on the computer case, then the monitor and finally any peripherals. Refer to the instructions included with your computer to confirm the precise procedure for your machine.

Several instructional books will have been provided to you by the computer manufacturer and enclosed with your new purchase. Feel free to sit back and read them at this time. Don't be surprised if you find them confusing—most people do. You can choose to read them in tandem with my instructions that follow or you can just go with my instructions and read the manufacturer's book later.

1. Find the "on" switch for your computer case. The "on" switch can usually be found on the front of the computer case under the floppy (A:) and CD-ROM (D:) drives. This switch will activate the operating system, keyboard and mouse. Press it, slide it, toggle it—whatever is the proper way to activate the switch. An indicator light, usually located on the front of the computer case, will light up when the unit is on (the keyboard may also have an indicator light, but the mouse will not). Give each computer component time to warm up—they don't always come to life immediately. Repeatedly pressing the "on" switch will only cause you and the computer to lose track of whether it's supposed to be on or off.

2. If the monitor is not on, turn it on. The "on" switch for a monitor is usually, but not always, located in the lower

front right corner of the monitor. Nothing will show on the monitor until the brain of the computer in the computer case is up and running. So sit tight and eventually something will appear on your monitor. If you can't find either "on" switches, refer to the instruction book that came with your machine.

3. If you bought yourself a printer, turn it on. The "on" switch can be located either at the front, back or side. Again, refer to the machine's literature if needed.

You may hear a sort of whirring or soft grinding sound as the hard drive in the computer case warms up. This can also be true throughout the time that you use the computer—the hard drive will periodically make a noise as it works. It's less disconcerting than it sounds and indicates that the computer is hard at work, which is a good thing.

Staying Turned On

If at any time you need to step away from the computer to answer the phone or run an errand, you can leave everything on without harming the machine. Some people never turn their computer off. In fact, it can actually be more harmful to turn the computer off and on frequently than to leave it on. Computers do, however, generate a certain amount of heat. If you plan to leave your machine on most of the time, make sure the area around the computer has good ventilation.

With a laptop, that means making sure there is circulation under the machine. If there are retractable legs on the bottom of the computer, use them to raise the computer. If not, use a small paperback or something similar under the back of the laptop to allow air circulation. This also angles the keyboard in a way that may be slightly more comfortable for you. Try it and see. However, I don't suggest leaving a laptop turned on indefinitely, as you might

It Isn't Working

One of the most common problems with computers is also the easiest to fix . . . believe it or not. If the screen is blank or the mouse or keyboard isn't working, check to make sure they are properly plugged into the computer case and wall outlet. Sounds too easy, but it's the case nine times out of ten.

If this isn't the case, leave the computer as it is and find help. Remember, if you've purchased a new machine, you're entitled to call for technical service under the warranty.

The Computer Will Not Explode

With earlier computers there was a lot of talk about them crashing and dying, which simply means the computer shuts off for no apparent reason and, in the worst case scenario, can't be turned on again.

Those earlier machines were much less durable than the ones today. It just isn't that easy to hurt your computer. If you treat it gently and be sure to read what's on the screen before you take an action, you'll do no damage.

"Crashing" and "dying" are unfortunate descriptives because they cause unnecessary anxiety. Chalk it up to dramatic excess and don't lose sleep over it.

a desktop. A laptop just doesn't get the same circulation as a desktop.

Note: The screen may appear different after you let it sit for a while. It may even seem that the computer has shut off. Some computer screens go into a standby, or "sleep" mode, or a screen saver may appear. (We'll talk more about screen savers in Chapter 12.) Simply move the mouse or hit any keyboard key to bring the screen back to life.

As I explained in Chapter 6, Macs and PCs have different operating systems (the mastermind that organizes everything in your computer) but all computers can do the same things—create documents, connect to the Internet, send e-mail, etc. However, there are different computer instructions for PCs and Macs. If you've bought a Mac, turn to page 119, and I'll join you there. If you've bought a PC, stay right where you are and keep reading. We'll all meet again on page 129.

Welcome, PC Users

As your computer starts up, your screen will remain dark and a series of startup messages will appear. They might appear and disappear so quickly that you can't read what they say. That's okay. If by chance you can read what they say, they won't make any sense anyway. This is a process the computer goes through to make sure everything is in working order.

● *The First Step*

If you're turning on a new PC for the very first time, there are some one-time-only setup procedures that you must go through.

Consult the *Getting Started* guide that came with your PC for what to do at this point. Read it along with these simplified instructions. You will most likely be instructed to type in the "Product ID or Product Key" number located on your Microsoft "Certificate of Authenticity" on the cover of the Microsoft book enclosed with your computer. Don't confuse the "Product ID" with the "Product Key." These are two different numbers. Be sure to double-check that you have typed in the correct number before going on to the next step. This information has to be *exactly* correct.

The appearance of an hourglass ⧗ in place of or along with the mouse's indicator arrow ▷ tells you that the computer is working on something and it is best not to use the keyboard or mouse until the hourglass goes away. For example, if you have just typed in your Product ID or Product Key number, the computer may take a moment to process that information; hence the hourglass, indicating that time is needed.

Identify Yourself

If you have Windows 98 or 2000, the next thing to appear on your screen will be titled **Enter Network Password.** If you have an older computer with Windows 95 as its operating system, you can skip this section.

Type your name in the top box next to the words **User name:**. If you want to have the first letters of your name capitalized, you need to use the **Shift** key, as you would on a typewriter. (There are two **Shift** keys—one near the bottom left of your keyboard, next to the Z key, and one on the right, next to the **? /** key. It doesn't matter which one you

Get Thee to a Computer

If you haven't purchased a computer yet but want to continue reading—*beware*. The book from this point forward is based on information that will appear on a computer screen. You will become *very* confused if you do not have a computer as a point of reference. Get yourself to someone's computer so you can follow along.

A Gentle Touch

If you hold down a key on the keyboard, it will keep ttttttttttyping. Use a quick depress and release to hit the key you want without having it rrrrrrepeat.

Oops—I Made a Mistake

If you make a mistake, you can erase your typing (from right to left) by using the **BkSp** (Backspace) key. (It can usually be found on the upper right section of your keyboard next to the + = key.) Depress it once for each letter that you want to erase. You'll see that it moves from right to left, deleting whatever precedes it on the screen. If you hold your finger down on the key, it will continue to move and delete to the left until you lift your finger. You definitely have more control when you depress and release the key with each character than when you hold the key down. If you want to delete from left to right, use the **Delete** or **Del** key on the keyboard.

use.) Depress **Shift** and hold it down as you type the letter that you want capitalized. If you make a mistake, use **BkSp**—the Backspace key. Remember to use the space bar to add a space between your first and your last name.

I don't advise that you enter a password in the box next to **Password:**. The password feature is really designed for computers that are part of a network or if you're going to have confidential information on your computer that you don't want anyone else to access. For the average at-home user, using a password means having to remember it and type it in every time you turn on the computer, which is unnecessary. So instead of typing anything in the box, depress the **Enter** key (on the right side of your keyboard next to the " ' key) and release. This will instruct the computer to accept that there is not a password.

Welcome to Windows

What appears next on your screen will be **Welcome to Windows**. In fact, **Welcome to Windows** is a wonderful introduction to your computer. It will appear on your screen every time you turn on the computer until you choose to deactivate it. We're not going to access anything here for now. You can go through the introduction the next time you turn on your computer. When you no longer want to have **Welcome to Windows** appear, move the mouse arrow to ☑ **Show this screen each time Windows starts** and click on the box. This will deactivate the window.

Don't be concerned if **Welcome to Windows** didn't appear on your screen. You should still read this section of the book to get familiar with your mouse. Of course, you won't be closing **Welcome to Windows**, as the instructions will ask, but otherwise you can follow along with my instructions.

Manipulating the Mouse

We're going to close **Welcome to Windows** so I can introduce you to the other items on your screen. To close it, you're going to use the mouse. Learning how to use the mouse is not unlike learning how to drive a standard-shift automobile. Do you remember how awkward it was trying to figure out when the clutch was in the right position to give the car gas or hit the brake? And do you remember how many times the car stalled before you got the clutch timing right? Well, welcome to the mouse. As you eventually conquered the clutch, you will eventually conquer the mouse. I promise.

Here we go. Take a look at **Welcome to Windows**. Do you see the blue bar at the top that says **Welcome to Windows**? That is called the **Title Bar**. In the right-hand corner of the Title Bar is an X enclosed in a small box ☒. That is the **Close Box**. Follow the instructions below to activate the Close Box and close **Welcome to Windows**. For those of you who don't have a **Welcome to Windows** window, complete steps 1 through 4. Read steps 5 and 6, but you won't be able to do them.

1. If you bought a desktop computer, gently rest your hand on the mouse with your index finger positioned over the button on the upper left side of the mouse. If you bought a laptop with a touchpad, trackball or touchpoint, place your index or middle finger on the pad, ball or point.

An Indicator Arrow by Any Other Name . . .

There are many names for what appears on your screen and moves according to how you manipulate the mouse. I tend to call it either the mouse arrow, the arrow or the mouse (example: move the mouse arrow to the happy face). You may find it called the pointer, indicator or cursor elsewhere. Whatever the name, it gets the job done.

Tension Is Your Enemy

There's no reason for you to feel any tension or strain in your hand. Manipulating the mouse is a task that requires accuracy, not strength. If you feel strain, your hand is not relaxed and it should be. You're probably concentrating too hard or your hand is in an awkward position. Use the illustration here as a guide for how to rest your hand properly on the mouse. Periodically stop what you're doing and focus on your hand. If you feel any strain, relax your hand and try a slightly different position.

2. *Slowly* move the mouse around on the mouse pad or your finger on the laptop mouse, and you'll notice that the arrow on the screen moves according to your manipulation of the mouse. If you have a desktop computer, lift the mouse off the mouse pad and move it around. You'll notice that when the ball on the bottom of the mouse doesn't have contact with a surface, there's no movement of the arrow on the screen. Place the

Whatever type of mouse you use, try to keep your hand relaxed and tension-free. It takes very little physical effort to move the mouse.

mouse back on the mouse pad. If you find yourself without enough surface space on the mouse pad, simply lift the mouse off the pad (your arrow will stay in place on the screen) and reposition it on the center of the pad.

3. Do *not* press any of the buttons on the mouse yet, and be careful not to accidentally put pressure on the mouse buttons while you move it around or you may click on and activate something unintentionally. If the mouse seems out of control, use very small hand or finger movements to make it move *much* slower. Over time you can go faster, but for now we are striving for optimum control of movement.

4. *Slowly* move the mouse arrow to the upper left corner of your screen. Now move it to the upper right, lower left and lower right corners. Did the arrow ever disappear off the edge of the screen? Sometimes that happens when you get close to the edge of the screen. No harm done—gently move the mouse around a bit and the arrow will reappear

on the screen. Don't ask me where it goes when this happens—it is the computer's version of hide-and-seek.

5. Now *slowly* move the mouse arrow to the ⊠ Close Box on **Welcome to Windows.** The tip of the mouse arrow needs to be *inside* the Close Box, not on the edge of the box. Keep your hand very steady so the arrow won't move from its position. If you're having trouble hitting your mark, take your hand off the mouse. Give your hand a rest, maybe shake it a bit. For some people this is easy, and for others it takes a few tries. When you're ready, try again.

6. Is the mouse arrow inside the ⊠ Close Box? *If you're using a desktop or an external mouse,* push on the button under your index finger and release. This is clicking the mouse. There may also be a button on the upper middle and right. I want you to depress *only* the button on the upper left. *If you're using a touchpad or trackball,* use your thumb to depress the button to the left of or above the pad or ball and release. *If you're using a touch point,* use your thumb to depress the top of the two buttons at the base of your computer. There is no need for the mouse to move when you depress the button.

Keep your eye on the screen and your hand steady.

If the **Welcome to Windows** box hasn't disappeared, there is nothing wrong with you or the computer; you simply didn't click the mouse correctly inside the ⊠ Close Box. Keep your eye on the mouse arrow on the screen and do not move the arrow when you depress the left button of the mouse. It's very common to move the mouse as you depress the button. That will unfortunately make the mouse click off-target. Keep trying—you'll get it eventually. Remember, it is like driving a car—keep your eye on the road (the screen), not the steering wheel (the mouse).

If you want to turn off the computer at any point, be sure to refer to the instructions on page 133. It is *very* important that the computer be shut down properly. My

66 In the beginning all sorts of things would appear on the screen and I couldn't figure out how they got there. As I calmed down and got more proficient with the mouse I realized I had been clicking on things without knowing it. 99

—Fred

advice is to leave the computer on and return to where you left off when you want to continue. There is no harm in leaving the computer on (the electricity costs are about the same as running a clock radio) and I don't want to have you jump ahead and miss some important instructions.

What About the Other Buttons on the Mouse?

For now I want you to depress only the upper left button of the mouse. The other buttons perform advanced actions that we aren't ready for. Be very careful not to let your fingers depress the buttons in the center or right by accident. Nothing bad will happen, but unfamiliar things will appear on your screen.

If something appears on your screen that you didn't intend to have there, either click on the ☒ Close Box as we just did or, if there is no Close Box, move the mouse to a blank space on the screen and click once with the left mouse button. That should get rid of whatever happened when you hit the wrong button.

The Windows Desktop

A non-laptop computer is called a "desktop" computer. The main screen display of your computer (whether it is on a desktop or laptop) is also called the "desktop." Isn't the English language a beautiful thing?

Your screen is now displaying the desktop. Think of it as the top of your desk in an office. From this screen you can access everything that your computer has to offer, just as you can access what you need on your office desk. The desktop is your home base.

First, find the brightness control on your monitor. It is most likely a dial somewhere on the bottom or side edge of the monitor. (Refer to your computer manual to locate it if

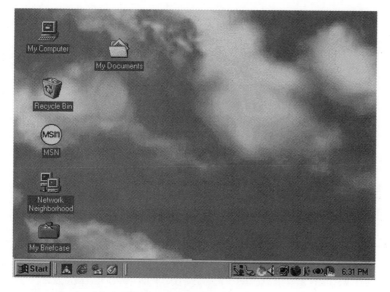

Your desktop screen may appear slightly different from this one, but it will offer the same basic features.

you can't find it.) Fiddle with the control until the brightness of the screen is right for you.

Your desktop screen may not exactly match the screen in the illustration. Each manufacturer configures how the desktop looks, so yours may have some of the same components, but they may appear slightly different.

The small pictures on your desktop are referred to as icons. These icons offer access to different programs and parts of your computer. They are like doors that you open by double-clicking on them. Instead of knock, knock to open the doors, you click, click or "double-click." You will get to know each of these icons and their capabilities in due time. But for now let's learn more about how to move about the computer.

EEK! It's a Mouse!

The mouse has a variety of functions. All of the tasks that the mouse performs are accomplished by moving the mouse to the designated area and depressing and releasing the button on the mouse.

In some ways it is more chameleon than mouse. You won't see its many mutations until later, but following are the different faces and what they mean.

What you see:	What it means:
⬉	This is the most common look for the mouse arrow. In this form it tells the computer where to take an action. When you move the mouse arrow, you need to be sure that the point of the arrow is on whatever you want to click on.
I	When you move the mouse arrow into a text area, it changes into an I-beam. This shape can be positioned easily between letters or numbers to mark where you want to make editing changes. This shape can be referred to as the cursor.
⧗	The hourglass icon indicates that the computer is busy performing a task. You shouldn't use the keyboard or the mouse until the hourglass changes back to an arrow.
⬉⧗	The combination of an hourglass and an arrow indicates that the computer is "multitasking," but you can still use the mouse. However, whatever you do may be slower than usual.
↕	An up-and-down arrow appears when the mouse is at the top or bottom edge of a window. This will allow you to click and drag to increase or decrease the height of the window.
↔	An arrow going right and left appears when the mouse is at the left or right edge of a window. This will allow you to click and drag to increase or decrease the width of the window.
⤢	A two-ended arrow at an angle appears when the mouse is at the corner of a window. This will allow you to click and drag so you can change the window's height and width.
☝	A hand with the index finger pointing indicates that if you press the mouse button, more information will become available. It is the *finger* of the hand that must be on the item desired—just as it is the point of the arrow.
⊘	A "don't" icon indicates that you're not allowed to take any action at this time. You're either in an area where you're prohibited from taking an action, or the computer is busy and will let you know when you can resume.

To Click or to Double-Click, That Is the Question

As I've said, to click the mouse means to depress and release one of its buttons. Clicking the mouse instructs the computer to perform a task (such as to open a document). You can click either the left button or the right button on the mouse, but you will never click them simultaneously. For now, however, unless I instruct you otherwise, you will use only the left button.

With the left button you can either single-click or double-click. A single click is accomplished by depressing and quickly releasing the button. To double-click, you depress, release, depress, release in quick succession. (The right button will only be a single click.)

There's no clear way to explain when to single- or double-click. Generally, you double-click on an icon to open it, allowing you to access an application software program. Remember, think of it as a knock, knock to allow entry to the program. Usually when you're in a program (typing a letter or playing a game), you single-click on something to perform a task. You'll get the feel for what's best to do when. If you single-click when a double click is necessary, you'll know because you won't accomplish your desired task. If you double-click when a single click is called for, nine times out of ten nothing is affected. On occasion the double click opens another window unexpectedly, but you can press **Esc** (Escape key—upper left on the keyboard) to correct things or click on the ☒ Close Box or a blank area on the screen to get rid of the unwanted window.

Let's Experiment

It's time to experiment with the mouse arrow on your desktop screen and become familiar with its movement.

1. Place your hand on the mouse (with the tail or cord of the mouse pointing away from you) and move the mouse

I Think I Can, I Think I Can, But Maybe I Can't Double-Click

It may be that double-clicking is giving you some trouble. You have a second option. When you're required to double-click to open an icon, you can single-click (to highlight the icon) and then depress and release the **Enter** key on your keyboard.

The Start Button Has Disappeared

If the **Start** button disappears, hold down the **Ctrl** key (bottom left on the keyboard) and the **Esc** key (upper left on the keyboard) at the same time and release. The **Start** button should reappear on your screen.

arrow to a blank space on the desktop screen. (Don't click on an icon yet.)

2. Click the left mouse button by depressing and releasing it with your finger.

3. Now depress and release the left button two times. Do it again as fast as you can. Continue double-clicking until you're comfortable with the action. For some, double-clicking can be tricky.

4. Once you've had enough of that, click once on the *right* button just for fun. The little gray box that appeared on the screen has advanced options that we don't want to get into yet. To get rid of the box, move the mouse arrow anywhere on a blank area of your desktop screen and click once with the *left* button.

If you get lost along the way or make an error, go back to step 1 and try again. You can also "click and drag" with the mouse. I don't want you to try this yet, but when it's time, we'll move the mouse arrow onto an item and "drag" the item to a new position on the screen. We'll practice this movement when we play Solitaire. But first we need to learn how to open the Solitaire window.

Place Your Bets

We're now going to open your Solitaire program, which is included in the Microsoft PC operating system. The **Start** button (at the bottom left of your screen) offers you access to everything on your computer, including any of your application software programs. It is also where you go to shut down the computer. Yes, you go to **Start** to stop the computer . . . don't ask me why. Follow the steps below to access Solitaire:

1. Move the mouse arrow to the **Start** button, located at the bottom left corner of your screen, and click once. *Remember, unless I instruct you otherwise, always click with the left button on your mouse.* What has now appeared on the screen is called the **Start Menu.** The Start Menu lists what is available on the computer.

To access Solitaire, you open a series of menu boxes. What appears on your screen may be slightly different from what you see here.

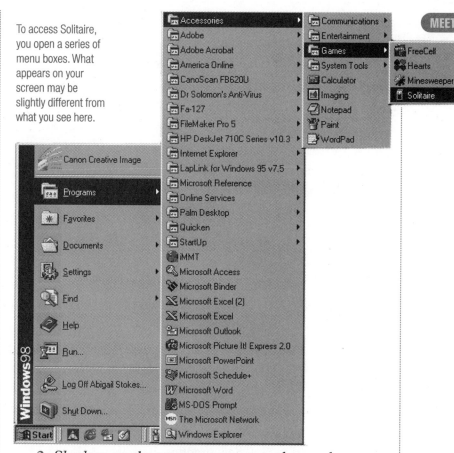

2. *Slowly* move the mouse arrow up to the word **Programs** ▶. You'll notice that if the arrow lingers as it passes over a word, that word becomes highlighted in blue, and if there is an arrow to the right of the word, a small gray box appears. Don't let this confuse you—keep moving the arrow up to the word **Programs** ▶. Stop when the arrow gets to the word **Programs** ▶. (You don't need to click the mouse. The blue highlighting shows the computer where you want to take an action.) In this case, we're going to open **Programs** ▶.

3. As soon as a gray box appears next to the word **Programs** ▶, *slowly* move the mouse arrow across the word **Programs** ▶ until it's in the gray box. Then move the arrow to the word **Accessories** ▶. Don't click the mouse yet. You'll notice that if you move too far up or down you

lose the desired gray box. Simply move the mouse back onto the area where you were and the box will reappear.

4. Another gray box will appear displaying **Accessories ▶** options. *Slowly* move the mouse arrow across the word **Accessories ▶** and onto the word **Games ▶**.

5. When the mouse arrow is on the word **Games ▶**, *slowly* move it across and into the gray box that contains the names of the games on your computer. Move to the word **Solitaire** and click the left button on the mouse once. At this point the Solitaire window should open.

If at any point you goof up and your mouse careens around the screen, don't worry. Just relax and try again. Move the mouse arrow to a blank spot on your desktop and click the left button once. That will make everything you opened from the **Start** button disappear. Return to step 1 on page 114 and begin again. If you opened another program by accident, move the mouse arrow to the ☒ Close Box and click once to get rid of it.

If that was rough going, don't despair. This is your first time playing with the mouse and accessing a program. It's all about practice, practice, practice. Keep repeating the steps above until you have opened the Solitaire window.

Learning the Parts of a Window

Look at the Solitaire window. The top blue bar, or the **Title Bar**, contains the name of the program you are now in. In this case it indicates that we are in the Solitaire window. The words in gray below the Title Bar are contained in the **Menu Bar**.

At the far right corner of the Title Bar are three small boxes. You remember that the ☒ to the far right is the Close Box. The box in the middle ☐ is the **Maximize Box**. And the box to the left ☐ is the **Minimize Box**.

These same features will appear on every window that you open on your computer. There will always be a Title Bar at the top that tells you which window you are viewing.

There will always be a Menu Bar, and a Close, a Maximize and a Minimize Box. Once you learn how to use these features within the Solitaire window, you will be able to use them on any window you open.

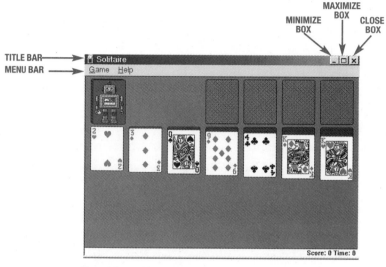

Every PC window has a Title Bar, Menu Bar, Minimize Box, Maximize Box and Close Box.

● *Maximize Box* 🗖

To maximize a window is to make the size of the window as large as possible. The advantage of this is that you will see more of what is contained in that window.

Move the mouse arrow into the 🗖 Maximize Box and click once. It's a little tricky to position the arrow exactly inside the box. If the Solitaire window disappears, you probably clicked the ☒ Close Box by accident. No harm done. Just go back to step 1 (page 114) and follow the instructions until you've reopened the Solitaire window. That's what we were going to do soon anyway—you get a little extra practice.

If you have successfully clicked on the 🗖 Maximize Box the Solitaire window will now take up the whole screen. It is maximized! Now look at the 🗖 Maximize Box. It has changed to look like this: 🗗. It has now become the **Restore Box**.

Why Are Some Letters Underlined?

Select letters within a word may be underlined on the screen. This underlining allows you to take the action associated with that word (i.e. opening a program or performing a task within a program) by using the keyboard rather than the mouse. You can do this by either depressing the letter on the keyboard that is underlined on the screen or by holding down the **Alt** key while you depress the letter on the keyboard. It varies how to activate the word, but you won't hurt anything by trying both methods.

Restore Box 🔲

To restore a window is to bring it back to its original size, which is smaller than when it is maximized. This allows you to view other items on the screen at the same time that you view part of what is contained in the restored window.

Move the mouse arrow onto the 🔲 Restore Box and click once to restore the Solitaire window to the size it was before you maximized it. Did the Solitaire window return to the size it was when you started? If the window disappeared, you might have clicked on one of the other boxes on the Title Bar instead. To catch up to where we are, go back to step 1 (page 114) and follow the instructions to reopen the Solitaire window. If it didn't disappear, you did it right.

Minimize Box 🔲

To minimize a window is to shrink the window to its smallest form and store it in the **Task Bar** at the bottom of your screen. The advantage of this is that you can access the window quickly but it isn't taking up space on your screen.

The Solitaire game is now minimized onto the Task Bar.

Let's see the Minimize Box in action. Move the mouse arrow onto the 🔲 and click once. If you click on the correct button, the box seems to disappear, but it doesn't really. You'll find a small gray box in the Task Bar at the bottom of your screen that contains the word **Solitaire**. This is the Solitaire window minimized.

The advantage of minimizing a window is that you can, in one click, get the window off the screen so you can view other items, then just click on it in the Task Bar to open it again. Return the window to its original size by moving the mouse arrow onto the word **Solitaire** and clicking once.

The Solitaire window is back on your screen.

Now, we're going to use the Close Box. Move the mouse arrow to the ☒ Close Box and click once. Goodbye, Solitaire window. Now go back to step 1 on page 114 and bring the Solitaire window back up on your screen, then meet me on page 129. It is the repetition and practice that will make you master of your computer.

Welcome, Mac Users

As your computer starts up, you will hear a "ding," perhaps more of a "bing"—you get the idea. That's the Mac's way of saying "hello." The first thing to appear on your screen is the Mac Picasso-esque logo with the words **Welcome to Mac OS** (OS stands for operating system). Next to appear are the words **Starting Up** with a box that fills in from left to right as the computer continues the startup process. The last thing to appear before the computer brings you to the desktop screen is a series of icons on the bottom of your screen. Each icon represents an extension or program in your computer.

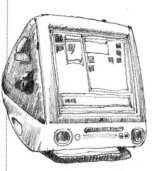

As the Mac starts up, the screen looks something like this.

The Mac Desktop

A non-laptop computer is called a "desktop" computer. The main screen display of your computer is also called the "desktop" (whether it is on a desktop or laptop). Isn't the English language a beautiful thing?

Your screen is now displaying the desktop. Think of it as

Note: If you have purchased an iMac you will have a round mouse. Most of my iMac students find this mouse difficult to manipulate. You have the option of purchasing an external mouse that is easier to manipulate. Make sure that your new mouse is Mac compatible.

the top of your desk in an office. From this screen you can access everything that your computer has to offer, just as you can access what you need on your office desk. The desktop is your home base.

While you are here, find the brightness control on your monitor. It is most likely a dial somewhere on the bottom or side edge of the monitor. (Refer to your computer manual to locate it if you can't find it.) Fiddle around with the control until the brightness of the screen is right for you. There is no standard about what is the appropriate brightness—it's what you find comfortable.

What you see in this illustration may not exactly match your screen. The small icons offer access to different programs and parts of your computer. They are like doors that you open by

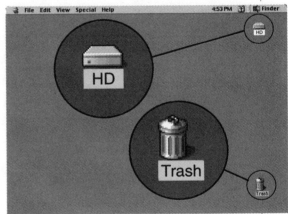

double-clicking on them. Instead of knock, knock to open the doors, you click, click or "double click." You will get to know each of these icons and their capabilities in due time. But for now let's learn more about how to move about the computer.

Manipulating the Mouse

Learning how to use the mouse is not unlike learning how to drive a standard-shift automobile. Do you remember how awkward it was trying to figure out when the clutch was in the right position to give the car gas or hit the brake? And do you remember how many times the car stalled before you got the clutch timing right? Well, welcome to the mouse. As you eventually conquered the clutch, you will eventually conquer the mouse. I promise. Let's try.

1. If you bought a desktop computer, gently rest your hand on the mouse with your index finger positioned over the button on the upper portion of the mouse. If you bought a laptop with a touchpad or trackball, place your index or middle finger on the pad or ball.

2. *Slowly* move the mouse or your finger around, and you'll notice that the arrow on the screen moves according to your manipulation of the mouse. If you have a desktop computer, lift the mouse off the mouse pad and move it around. You'll notice that when the ball on the bottom of the mouse doesn't have contact with a surface, there's no movement of the arrow on the screen. Place the mouse back on the mouse pad. If you find you don't have enough surface space on the mouse pad, simply lift the mouse off the pad (your arrow will stay in place on the screen) and reposition the mouse on the center of the pad.

3. Do *not* press any of the buttons on the mouse yet, and be careful not to accidentally put pressure on the button of the mouse while you move it around. If the mouse seems out of control, use very small hand or finger movements to make it move *much* slower. Over time you can go faster, but for now we are striving for optimum control of movement.

4. *Slowly* move the mouse arrow to the upper left corner of your screen. Now move it to the upper right, lower left and lower right corners. Did the arrow ever disappear off the edge of the screen? Sometimes that happens when you get close to the edge of the screen. No harm done—gently move the mouse around a bit and the arrow will reappear on the screen. Don't ask me where it goes when this happens—it's the computer's version of hide-and-seek.

5. Now slowly move the mouse arrow to the word **File** at the top left of your screen. *If you're using a desktop computer or an external mouse,* depress the button under your index finger. *If you're using a touchpad or trackball,* use your thumb to depress the button to the left of or above the pad or ball and release.

Tension Is Your Enemy

There's no reason for you to feel any tension or strain in your hand. Manipulating the mouse is a task that requires accuracy, not strength. If you feel strain, your hand is not relaxed and it should be. You're probably concentrating too hard or your hand is in an awkward position. Use the illustration here as a guide for how to rest your hand properly on the mouse. Periodically stop what you're doing and focus on your hand. If you feel any strain, relax your hand and try a slightly different position.

In the beginning all sorts of things would appear on the screen and I couldn't figure out how they got there. As I calmed down and got more proficient with the mouse I realized I had been clicking on things without knowing it.

—Fred

There is no need for the mouse to move when you depress the button. *Keep your eye on the screen and your hand steady.*

6. While the button remains depressed, move the mouse arrow onto the words **New Folder,** then release the button. Keep your hand very steady so the arrow won't move from its position. If you're having trouble hitting your mark, take your hand off the mouse. Give your hand a rest, maybe shake it a bit. For some people this is easy, and for others it takes a few tries. When you're ready, try again.

7. When you release the mouse button, a new icon looking like a file folder with the words **untitled folder** enclosed in a box below should appear on the screen. We need to open this folder to produce a window. Move the mouse arrow onto the folder itself (not the words below) and depress the mouse button and release. The folder should now be highlighted.

8. Move the mouse arrow back up to the word **File** (at the top left of the screen). Depress the mouse button and hold it down as you move the mouse arrow down to the word **Open**. Once you have highlighted the word **Open**, release the button. You have just opened a window on your computer screen!

9. Now we're going to close the window. Find the ☐ box in the upper left corner of the window. This is the **Close Box**. Move the mouse arrow *inside* the ☐ Close Box. It is important that the tip of the arrow is *inside* the Close Box, not on the edge of the box. Keep your hand steady so the mouse won't move from its position. Depress and release your mouse button. The **untitled folder** window has now disappeared. Well done.

If the box hasn't disappeared, there is nothing wrong with you or the computer; you simply didn't click the mouse correctly inside the ☐ Close Box. Keep your eye on the mouse arrow on the screen and do not move the arrow when you depress the left button of the mouse. It's very common to move the mouse as you depress the button. That will unfortunately make the mouse click off-target. Keep trying—you'll get it eventually. Remember it is like driving a car—keep your eye on the road (the screen), not the steering wheel (the mouse).

If you want to turn off the computer at any point, be sure to refer to the instructions on page 133. It is *very* important that the computer be shut down properly. My advice instead is to leave the computer on and return to where you left off when you want to continue. There is no harm in leaving the computer on, and I don't want to have you jump ahead and miss some important instructions.

EEK! It's a Mouse!

The mouse has a variety of functions. All of the tasks that the mouse performs are accomplished by moving the mouse to the designated area and depressing the button.

In some ways it is more chameleon than mouse. You won't see its many mutations until later, but following are the different faces and what they mean:

The Name Game

There are many names for what appears on your screen and moves according to how you manipulate the mouse. I tend to call it either the mouse arrow, the arrow or the mouse. Elsewhere you may find it called the pointer, indicator or cursor. Whatever the name, it gets the job done.

What it means:	What you see:
This is the most common look for the mouse arrow. In this form it tells the computer where to take an action. When you move the mouse arrow, you need to be sure that the point of the arrow is on whatever you want to click on.	
When you move the mouse arrow into a text area, it changes into an I-beam. This shape can be positioned easily between letters or numbers to mark where you want to make editing changes. This shape can be referred to as the cursor.	
This clock symbol indicates that the computer is busy performing a task. You shouldn't use the keyboard or the mouse until the clock changes back to an arrow.	
A hand with the index finger pointing indicates that if you press the mouse button, more information will become available. This configuration is seen often when you're on the Internet. It is the finger of the hand that must be on the item desired—just as it is with the point of the arrow.	

To Click or to Double-Click, That Is the Question

As I've said before, to click the mouse means to depress and release the button. Clicking the mouse instructs the computer to perform a task (such as open a document). This can take a single or a double click. A single click is accomplished by depressing and then quickly releasing the button. To double-click, you depress, release, depress, release in quick succession.

There is no clear way to explain when to single- or double-click. Generally, you double-click on an icon to open it, allowing you to access an application software program. Remember, think of it as a knock, knock to allow entry to the program. Usually when you're in a program (typing a letter or playing a game), you single-click on something to perform a task. You'll get the feel for what's best to do when. If you single-click when a double-click is necessary, you'll know because you won't accomplish your desired task. If you double-click when a single click is called for, nine times out of ten nothing is affected. On occasion the double click opens another window unexpectedly, but you can press **Esc** (Escape key—upper left on the keyboard) to correct things or click on the ☐ Close Box or a blank area on the screen to get rid of the unwanted window.

Let's Experiment

It's time to experiment with the mouse arrow on your desktop screen to become familiar with its movement.

1. Place your hand on the mouse (with the tail or cord of the mouse pointing away from you) and move the mouse arrow to a blank space on the desktop screen. (Don't click on an icon yet.)

2. Click the mouse button by depressing and releasing it with your finger.

3. Now depress and release the mouse button two times. Try it again and do it as fast as you can. Continue double-

---

I Think I Can, I Think I Can, But Maybe I Can't Double-Click

It may be that double clicking is giving you some trouble. You have a second option. When you're required to double-click to open an icon, you can single-click (to highlight the icon). Then move the mouse arrow onto the word **File** at the top left of your screen. Depress the mouse button and keep it depressed while you move down to the word **Open**. Once you are on the word **Open**, release the mouse.

clicking until you're comfortable with the action. For some, double-clicking can be kind of tricky.

You can also "click and drag" with the mouse. I don't want you to try this yet, but when it's time we'll move the mouse arrow onto an item and "drag" the item to a new position on the screen. Let's go play around a bit, and I'll show you what I mean.

● *Learning the Parts of a Window*

Reopen the **untitled folder** that you created on page 122 by moving the mouse onto the folder (not the words below) and double-clicking. If you are having trouble with the double click, you can single-click on the folder to highlight it, then click on the word **File** at the top left and single-click on the word **Open**. Your **untitled folder** window should now be open.

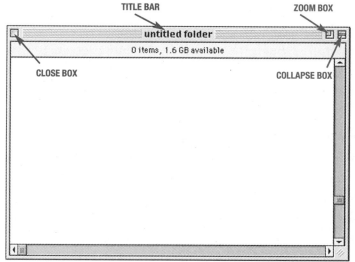

Every Mac window has a Title Bar, Close Box, Zoom Box and Collapse Box.

Look at the window. The words at the top of the screen are contained in the **Title Bar**. In the far left corner of the Title Bar is the ☐ Close Box. In the right corner of the Title Bar are two more boxes. The box on the left is the ⊟ **Zoom Box** and the box to the right is the ⊟ **Collapse Box**. There is also the ⌗ **Size Box** (sometimes called the

66I thought I would never be able to control the mouse. It took me a long time to feel comfortable with the clicking and the movement. I made a lot of mistakes along the way, but eventually it got easier. Sometimes I don't even think about it now— I just do it.99

—Eileen

Grow Box) in the bottom right corner. (We'll go over this later.)

These same features will appear on every window that you open on your computer. There will always be a Title Bar at the top that tells you which window you are viewing. There will always be a Menu Bar, a Close Box, Zoom Box and Collapse Box. Once you learn to use these features in this window, you will be able to use them on any window.

Zoom Box ⬜

When you use the Zoom Box, it makes the size of the window as large as possible. The advantage of this is that you will see more of what is contained in that window.

Move the mouse arrow to the ⬜ Zoom Box and click once. It's a little tricky to position the arrow exactly inside the box. If you've successfully clicked on the Zoom Box, you'll see that the **untitled folder** window now takes up the whole screen. Note: Sometimes the window thinks it's maximized, but it isn't taking up the entire screen. In that case the window can be maximized by using the ▨ Size Box. We'll play with the Size Box later.

To restore the **untitled folder** window to the size it was when you started, move the arrow back onto the ⬜ Zoom Box and click once. If the window is now the original size, you did it right.

Collapse Box ⊟

When you use the Collapse Box, it shrinks the window to its smallest form. The advantage of this is that you can access the window quickly but it isn't taking up space on your screen.

Let's see the Collapse Box in action. Move the mouse arrow onto the ⊟ Collapse Box and click once. If it seems as though the box has disappeared, leaving behind only the Title Bar, you have successfully collapsed the window. To restore the window to its original size, move the mouse arrow onto the ⊟ Collapse Box and click once. The **untitled folder** window is back on your screen.

● *Close Box* ☐

To close the window completely, move the mouse arrow into the ☐ Close Box and click once. Goodbye, **untitled folder** window. If that was rough going, don't worry. This is your first time playing with the mouse. It's all about practice, practice, practice.

● *Puzzling*

Unlike a PC with a Microsoft operating system, a Mac doesn't come with Solitaire pre-installed on the hard drive. Instead, we will use the jigsaw puzzle that came with your Mac to learn how to click and drag the mouse. If you

purchased Solitaire software when you bought your computer, you can either use the puzzle that came installed on your Mac or you can skip this section and go directly to "Place Your Bets" (page 128) to play Solitaire.

It isn't my intention for you to become a puzzle nut. What I really want you to do is master the mouse. Your homework is

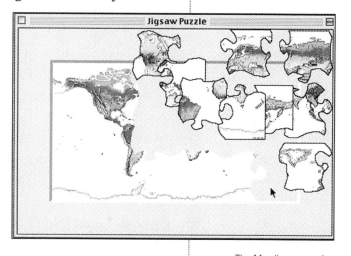

The Mac jigsaw puzzle.

to play with the jigsaw puzzle as much as you can. Once the mouse is your slave, go on to the next chapter. Remember, it is practice and only practice that will allow you to conquer the mouse or any other aspect of the computer.

To access the jigsaw puzzle:

1. Move the mouse arrow up to the ● Apple logo at the top left of the screen.

2. Click on the Apple logo but keep your finger depressed on the mouse button while you move the arrow down to the words **jigsaw puzzle**. Release the mouse button.

3. The jigsaw puzzle window should now be on the screen.

In order to move a piece of the puzzle, you must click and drag it. Place the mouse arrow on the puzzle piece you want to move. Press down on the mouse button and, without lifting your finger, move the mouse arrow to where you want the puzzle piece placed. Once the piece is exactly where you want it to be, let go of the button on the mouse.

Is There More?

For the fun of it, if you move the mouse arrow up to the word **Options**, several different options become available.

• Click once on **start new puzzle**. At this point you are given the choice of staying with the puzzle pieces as they are now or changing their size to larger or smaller.

• Click on whichever size you want to try.

• You can also change the background color of the jigsaw puzzle window. Click once on **set background color**, then click on the color you desire. Once you have made your decision, click on **OK**.

Place Your Bets

If you aren't going to play Solitaire, skip to **Ready to Call it a Day?** on page 133.

You can try to install the Solitaire software following the instructions that came with it. But if it seems too hard, don't hesitate to call and ask someone who has a computer to help you.

Once the software is installed, open your Solitaire program using the following steps:

1. If there is a Solitaire icon on your desktop screen,

move the mouse arrow onto the icon and double-click. It is important that the arrow be on the icon and not on the words below.

2. If there isn't an icon, move the mouse arrow to your 🖴 Hard Disk icon and double-click.

3. Find the **Application** folder. Move the mouse arrow onto that folder and double-click.

4. Now find the **Solitaire** folder. Move the mouse arrow onto that folder and double-click. The Solitaire window is now opened.

PC and Mac Card Sharks, Unite!

So here we are with the **Solitaire** window opened. Let's review the rules of Solitaire and then we can play a hand. If you already know how to play Solitaire, skip this section and we'll catch up with you at "How Do the Cards Get Moved?" (page 131).

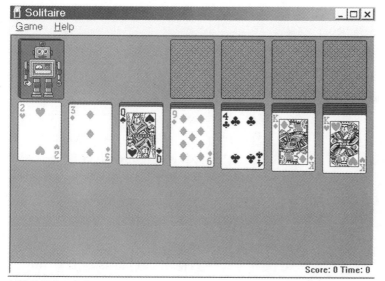

A PC Solitaire window.

Trivia

There are many versions of Solitaire and many names for each game. The familiar version is often called Klondike. It most likely dates back to the Klondike gold rush in the late 19th century.

Mac Users: Aversion to Different Versions

Your version of Solitaire may differ slightly from what we have described here. This is true of any software package. Follow my instructions as best you can, but when in doubt refer to your software manual.

• The ultimate goal of Solitaire is to have all the cards in four piles in the empty spots of the Solitaire window. Each stack must be of a single suit and in ascending order, with the ace on the bottom and the king on top (ace, 2, 3 . . . jack, queen, king).

• Along the way, your challenge is to build on the cards that are face up in the seven piles. You add cards to these piles moving down in value (10, 9, 8 . . .) but you must alternate in color (black, red, black, red).

• You can play the top card in any of the seven piles or play the card that is face up in the draw pile. When you take a card from the draw pile, the card below will be revealed and may then be played.

• As you use a card from the seven piles, the card below it can be played. If an empty space is

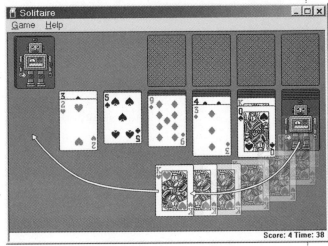

Score: 4 Time: 38

A king is the only card that can be moved to an empty space.

created, only a king can be moved to that spot; then you can start building on the king in the same way the other piles are built (king, queen, jack . . . alternating red and black).

• If you come upon an ace, move it to one of the open four spots and build up your stacks by suit (ace, 2, 3 . . .).

• A series of cards can be moved together. Example: If you have a

Aces are moved to the spaces at the top right of the window.

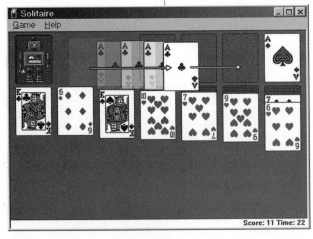

Score: 11 Time: 22

black queen revealed in one pile and in another stack you

have built a series with a red jack, black 10 and red 9, you can move the series, starting with the red jack onto the black queen.

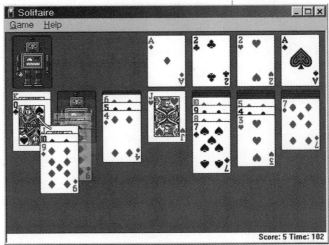

• Keep in mind, the strategy in Solitaire is to try to expose as many face-down cards as possible.

A series of cards can be moved together by clicking on the highest card of the series and dragging it to the appropriate spot. All the cards in the series will move together.

Don't get frustrated if you don't often win. If you win one out of five games you're doing quite well. Remember: It isn't whether you win or lose, it's how you control the mouse.

How Do the Cards Get Moved?

In order to move a card, you must click and drag it. Place the mouse arrow on the card that you want to move. Press the mouse button and, without lifting your finger, drag the card to where you want it to be. Then let go of the button on the mouse.

To flip over a card from the draw pile, move the mouse arrow onto the card and click once. If you double-click here you will turn over two cards, so be careful.

Let the Games Begin

Look at the cards that are face up in your seven piles.

If there is an ace, move the mouse arrow onto the ace. Press down the mouse button. With the mouse button held down, move the card onto one of the four designated blank spots. Take your finger off the mouse button. If this didn't work, give it another try.

Huh? What Happened?

You'll discover that the computer will not allow you to make a mistake or cheat! If you choose a card and try to play it on another card incorrectly, the computer will send your choice flying back to its original spot as soon as you release the mouse button.

Click and Drag . . . Is It a Drag?

Are you having some trouble with the click and drag maneuver? Let's review:

- Place the mouse arrow on the object you want to move and depress the mouse button.
- Keep the mouse button depressed while you drag the object by moving the mouse to where you desire.
- Take your finger off the mouse and the object will remain where it has been moved.

My advice is, *keep playing Solitaire!* It may seem silly (or drive you nuts), but it is the best way to master the mouse. If you haven't been faithfully doing your homework, start today!

Look for a card one less in number than any of the cards face up. Is the color different? (They must alternate black and red or vice versa.)

- If you have a card to move, move the mouse arrow to that card and click and drag the card to its new position.
- If you don't have a card to move, can you play the face-up card in the draw pile?
- If you can't play that card, click once on the face-down pile. Can you use that card? Keep flipping cards until there's a card to play. If the draw pile is depleted, click once on the empty area so you can go through the pile again.

The game continues like this until you can't play any of the cards available to you. Unfortunately, that means you've lost. But perhaps you've completed the four piles by suit from ace to king. That means you've won.

If you want to play again, move the mouse arrow onto the word **Game** in the Menu Bar and click once. Now move the arrow down to the word **Deal** and click again.

Remember the Goal

Play Solitaire for at least half an hour every day for a week. If you choose to play more, make sure you take five-minute breaks every half hour or so. What you are really doing is mastering the mouse. Once the mouse is your slave, go on to the next chapter. Remember, it is practice and only practice that will allow you to conquer the mouse or any other aspect of the computer.

Exit Solitaire

If you have a PC, move your mouse arrow to the ☒ Close Box of the Solitaire window and click once.

If you have a Mac, move your mouse arrow to **File** and click once. If the **File** window doesn't remain open, hold down the mouse button. Then move the mouse arrow down to the word **Quit** or **Close** and click once.

Ready to Call it a Day?

The computer *always* needs to be shut down properly. You must try to avoid turning the power off instead of going through the shut-down process. If you do not go through the proper shut-down procedures, you can damage the computer. It is best to close all the windows that are open and quit any programs that you are in. If you forget to do this, the computer will remind you.

● *Putting the Computer to Bed*

If you have a PC:

1. Move your mouse arrow to the **Start** button in the bottom left corner of your screen and click once.

2. Move your mouse arrow up to the words **Shut Down** and click once. The **Shut Down Windows** window will appear. Make sure that the circle next to the words **Shut Down** is filled in. If not, move the mouse to the words **Shut Down** and click once.

3. Now you have a choice. You can either hit the **Enter** key or move the mouse arrow to the word **OK** or **Yes** and click once. Both will instruct the computer to shut down.

4. Once your screen says **It is now safe to turn off your computer,** wait a moment to see if it shuts off automatically; if not, you can turn the power source off. Some computers will automatically shut off after the **Please wait while your computer shuts down** screen turns black.

5. Also turn off anything else that may still be on—your monitor, the printer, etc.

If you have a Mac:

1. Move your mouse arrow to the word **Special** and depress the mouse button, then to the words **Shut Down**

and release the mouse button. This will instruct the computer to shut down.

2. Turn off anything else that may still be on—your monitor, the printer, etc.

If You Have a Laptop:

Whether you have a Mac or a PC, be sure to close the cover after completing the above steps.

Hurrah!

That was a huge amount to accomplish! If you are bleary-eyed you are not alone. We covered a lot of material for your initiation, but initiated you are!

When you want to come back to the computer, you can repeat any or all of this chapter. What you *must* do is open the Solitaire window (or jigsaw puzzle for Mac users) and play for at least half an hour every day for a week. I want you to be skilled with the mouse and have an understanding of your options within a window. At the end of that time, you'll never have to do it again unless you want to.

■ LET'S REVIEW

Below is a quick guide to get you up and running with Solitaire (or the jigsaw puzzle for Mac users).

If you are using a PC

TO ACCESS SOLITAIRE:

- Turn on the computer and wait for it to warm up.
- If the **Network Password** window appears, depress **Enter**.
- Close whatever windows appear.
- Move the mouse arrow to the **Start** button and click.
- Move the mouse arrow up to **Programs** and across to **Accessories**.

Don't Despair

If you purchased a laptop computer and you continue to have trouble manipulating the pad, ball or point mouse, you have the option of purchasing an external mouse. Make sure that your new mouse is compatible with either your PC or Mac.

- Move the mouse arrow across **Accessories** and onto **Games**.

- Move the mouse arrow across **Games** and onto **Solitaire**, then click once. Have fun!

TO SHUT DOWN:

- Close the **Solitaire** window and any other windows that are open.

- Move the mouse arrow to the **Start** button and click.

- Move the mouse arrow up to the words **Shut Down** and click.

- Either hit **Enter** or move the mouse to **OK** or **Yes** and click once.

If you are using a Mac

TO ACCESS THE JIGSAW PUZZLE:

- Turn on computer and wait for it to warm up.

- Click on the ■ Apple logo on the Menu Bar.

- Click on **jigsaw puzzle**.

TO ACCESS SOLITAIRE:

- Double-click on the **Solitaire** icon on your desktop or if you don't have a **Solitaire** icon:

1. Double-click on the **Hard Disk** icon.

2. Double-click on the **Applications** folder.

3. Double-click on the **Solitaire** folder.

TO SHUT DOWN:

- Close the **Solitaire** window, **jigsaw puzzle** window and any other windows that are open.

- Move your mouse arrow to the word **Special** and depress the mouse button.

- Move the mouse arrow to the words **Shut Down** and release the mouse button.

12

Getting to Know You
Experimenting with what you can do on the computer

In the last chapter you were introduced to the mouse. This chapter will introduce you to the Mac and PC operating systems, as well as to some other features that your computer has to offer. Mac users turn to page 152. PC users continue reading. But remember, don't sit at the computer too long without taking a break. Also check the position of your back, arms and legs in relation to the computer and review the ergonomic safety tips on page 99.

Welcome, PC Users

Turn on your computer. As you know by now, if the **Welcome to Windows** window appears, click on the ☒ **Close Box** to close it. The desktop screen should appear. In this chapter we will customize some features on your computer and investigate a few others. Feel free to move at your own pace. You can stop and start wherever and whenever you want.

● *My Computer* My Computer

Let's open some of the icons on the desktop screen and see specifically what they have to offer. First we'll open the icon

When you open an icon or folder, it's important that the arrow is placed on the icon and not on the text description below the icon.

When All Else Fails

If you absolutely cannot double-click, there is a solution. Single-click on the icon. Now that the icon is highlighted you can depress and release the **Enter** key to open the icon.

labeled **My Computer**. The **My Computer** window allows access to both the software and hardware on your computer. From here you can get to all the information stored on your hard drive, as well as the A: and D: drives which hold your floppy and CD-ROM disks.

Move the mouse arrow onto the 🖥 **My Computer** icon and double-click. If the icon is highlighted in blue but the window didn't open, your double click wasn't successful. Place the mouse arrow on the icon again and depress, release, depress, release the mouse button in as rapid succession as you can. Think knock, knock. Keep trying, and eventually you will get the timing.

As I describe each icon

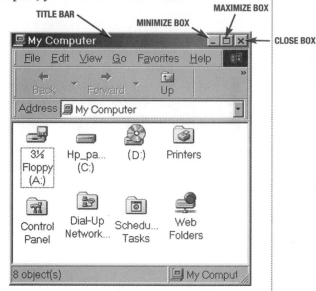

The "My Computer" window. Notice that it has a Title Bar, and Minimize, Maximize and Close Boxes. Most PC windows have these features.

contained in the **My Computer** window, feel free to double-click on the icon to open it and see what's inside. To get back to the **My Computer** window, move the mouse arrow to the word **Back** on the upper left side of the Menu Bar and click once. If you have somehow closed the window, simply find the **My Computer** icon on the desktop screen and double-click on it to reopen it.

The 🖳 **3 1/2 Floppy (A:)** icon allows you to see what is on a floppy disk in your A: drive. When the time comes, you'll insert a floppy disk into the A: drive, then double-click on the icon. From that point, whatever is on the disk can be accessed. If you double-click on the icon when there

isn't a floppy disk in the A: drive, you will see a very
ominous message:

The message's bark
is bigger than its bite;
to get rid of it, either
move the mouse
arrow to the ⊠
Close Box or to the
word **Cancel** and
click once.

This warning appears when
you click on the A: drive icon
without having a floppy disk
in the A: drive.

The ▭ (C:) icon allows access to anything on your
computer's C: drive. Because the C: drive is the storage
space for everything on your computer, you can find
anything you need through this icon.

Find a folder titled **My Documents** in the C: drive.
That folder will store whatever writing you eventually do
on the computer. You probably won't be able to see all that
is contained in the C: drive, but if you click on the ▣
Maximize Box, you will be able to see more of what's in the
window. Later I will explain how to view the entire contents
of a window (page 142).

The 🖳(D:) icon (also referred to as **E:**) allows you to
hear and/or see a compact disc or CD-ROM on your
computer. When a CD-ROM or a music CD is in the D:
drive, this icon will offer you choices about which track you
may want to listen to and the volume you prefer. We will
experiment with this later in the chapter.

The 🗀 **Printers** icon allows you access to both the
printer you're already using and a new printer that you
might add at any time. This is also the place to go if you
change your mind once you start printing a document and
want to stop the printer (or "purge print documents" in
computer-speak).

The 🗀 **Dial-Up Networking** icon is something you
will probably never use. This is where the dialing system is
set up for your access to the Internet. If at some point you

decided to reconfigure your dial-up networking, you would double-click on this icon to access the area where you would make those changes.

The 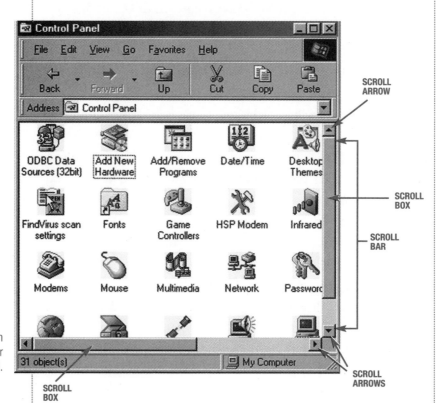 **Control Panel** icon allows you to access almost every feature of your computer and to customize it to your needs. We'll stay here for a while and explore some of the options available. So if you haven't already done it, double-click on the **Control Panel** icon.

What's in the Window?

The size of the window dictates how much of the information it contains is visible to you. This is where the **Scroll Bar** comes in handy. The Scroll Bar allows you to move the information in the window up and down for full viewing.

You can customize certain parts of your computer using the Control Panel.

You will notice that this window has the same features as the Solitaire window. It has a Title Bar, Menu Bar, ▬ Minimize Box, ☐ Maximize Box and ☒ Close Box. What we haven't discussed yet is the Scroll Bar on the bottom and right side of the window.

If you see a Scroll Bar on the right edge or bottom of a window, this tells you that there is more in the window than you can see. (If there is no Scroll Bar on the window of your screen, don't worry. On page 142 there are instructions on how to make a Scroll Bar appear.) You can increase the size of the window or scroll the window to see what else it contains. Students often call me in distress because they can't find an item that they know is supposed to be in a certain window. Usually it is right where it should be, but they didn't see all the contents of the window. The Scroll Bar is your clue that there is more to be unveiled.

Enlarging the Window The most efficient way to see all the contents of a window is to increase its size. You can do that in a number of ways. For the sake of experimentation, try each option. Once you have seen how each choice works, follow the instructions in italics to restore the window and go on to the next option. We will experiment with scrolling after you have tried the following options.

Option 1. There is a box in the Title Bar that will increase the size of the window. Do you remember which box that is? Correct! The 🔲 Maximize Box. Move the mouse arrow into the 🔲 and click once. *To restore it back to its original form, move the mouse arrow to the 🔲 **Restore Box** and click once.*

Option 2. Move your mouse arrow to the bottom right corner of the Control Panel window. Your arrow will become a two-ended arrow at an angle ↘ . (If the double arrow eludes you it is because you are moving the mouse too quickly—slow down.) As you did with the Solitaire cards, click and drag the arrow to the bottom right of your screen, then release the mouse button. *To restore, place the mouse arrow in the bottom right corner of the window to activate the two-ended arrow. Now click and drag the corner to the left and up until the window is the size it was when you first opened it.*

It is a delicate business to get the mouse arrow exactly on the edge of the window to activate the arrows that will allow you to stretch or shrink it. Move the mouse VERY slowly and you'll get the hang of it. Be patient and don't give up.

Click and Drag . . . Is It a Drag?

Are you having some trouble with the click and drag maneuver? Let's review:

- Place the mouse arrow on the object you want to move and depress the mouse button.
- Keep the mouse button depressed while you drag the object (by moving the mouse) to where you desire.
- Take your finger off the mouse and the object will remain where it has been moved.

My advice is, *if you have Solitaire, keep playing.* It may seem silly (or drive you nuts), but it is the best way to master the mouse. If you haven't been faithfully doing your homework, start today!

Option 3. Move the mouse arrow to the right side of the Control Panel window. The arrow now becomes an arrow going right and left ↔. Click and drag the arrow to the far right edge of the screen and then release the mouse button. This increases the width. (The same can be done with the left side of the window.) To increase the height, move the right-left arrow to the bottom of the window. Now the mouse arrow becomes an up and down arrow ↕. Click and drag the arrow to the far bottom edge of the screen and then release the mouse. (The same can be done with the top of the window.) *To restore, place the mouse arrow on the right of the screen to activate the arrow going right and left. Now click and drag the edge to the left until the window is about the width it was when you first opened it. Do the same with the bottom edge of the window.*

● Scrolling Along

There can be more contained in a window than can be seen no matter how large you make the window. In this case, you will have to use the Scroll Bar to see all that is available. The Scroll Bar is similar to an elevator: a button is pressed to activate it, it moves up and down and you can get off anyplace you want.

Does your window look something like the window seen here? Make sure that there is a Scroll Bar on the right side of the window.

If you see a Scroll Bar, it indicates that you're not seeing everything in the window.

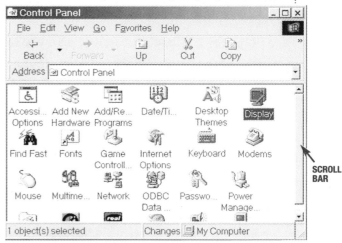

SCROLL BAR

If there isn't a Scroll Bar, move the mouse arrow onto the lower right corner of the window. It will now be the two-sided arrow at an angle ⬊ . Click and drag the corner up and left to create a Scroll Bar on the right side and bottom of the window.

There should be a set of arrows at the top and bottom of the Scroll Bar positioned on the right edge of the window. If there is a Scroll Bar at the bottom of the window, it will also have a set of arrows positioned at the right and left. Now let's take a scroll . . .

- Place the mouse arrow on the bottom ▼ scroll arrow on the right edge of the window and click a few times. With each click the image on the screen moves down. *Be careful that the mouse arrow stays within the box that contains the scroll arrow. If your mouse wanders, you will not be able to activate the Scroll Bar, or the window may scroll in increments greater than you desire.*

- The contents within the window will move up if you place the mouse arrow on the top ▲ scroll arrow and click.

- The window will scroll left or right with the bottom ◀ left and ▶ right scroll arrows.

- If you hold down the mouse button rather than depressing and releasing it, the window will scroll very quickly. This technique is more difficult to control, but faster than individual clicks.

- You can also reveal what's inside the window by placing the mouse arrow on the **Scroll Box** within the Scroll Bar and clicking and dragging the Scroll Box up or down. This is faster than using the scroll arrows and is most convenient if you're in a very large document wanting to get from, for example, page 1 to page 40.

Scroll Bars play a big role in web sites on the Internet. I strongly recommend that you spend time maneuvering a Scroll Bar every time you play on the computer until you have the technique down.

“For the longest time I couldn't use the Scroll Bar. I kept moving the mouse off the arrow or clicking too fast. Eventually it became easier. You really can't take advantage of web sites without it.”
—Dan

Does Anybody Really Know What Time It Is?

Maximize the Control Panel window if you can't see all the icons contained in it. (Remember, you do that by clicking on ▣.) We're going to be sure that the date and time are set properly on your computer. Once set, the computer, even when it is shut off, will keep perfect time and the current date. Open the **Date/Time** window by double-clicking on the ▦ Date/Time icon.

At the bottom of the Control Panel window there are three buttons: **OK, Cancel** and

This window allows you to set the date and time.

Apply. These are your action choices. Sometimes a window will offer you **Help, Yes** or **No** as choices. When you click on any of these buttons, you're instructing the computer to take that action. You must be *very sure* of the action you want to take—sometimes it is irreversible.

Notice that the box containing **OK** has a slightly darker outline. In this case the computer assumes **OK** to be the most likely choice for you. Be forewarned, if you depress the **Enter** key on your keyboard, whatever action the computer has selected will be taken. *That is why it is so important not to arbitrarily depress the* **Enter** *key; you may unwittingly take an action that cannot be reversed.* (Note: It may not be OK if the computer preselects for you. It could be any action button that the computer deems will be your likely choice.) In the case of what we are playing with here, not to worry—nothing is irreversible.

Follow the steps below to adjust the date and time on your computer:

- Click once on the **Time Zone** tab.
- There is a box highlighted in blue below the tab with an ▼ arrow to the right. Is the time zone that is visible your time zone? If not, click on the arrow. Find your time zone (the Scroll Bar may have to be used), point on it with the mouse arrow and click once.
- Does **Automatically adjust clock for daylight saving changes** have a check ☑ in the box to the left? If not, move the mouse arrow to the box and click once. Yes, like magic your computer will make the adjustment for daylight savings from now on! Adjust your screen brightness if you have difficulty seeing the map.
- At this point click once on the word **Apply** or **Set**. This instructs the computer to accept your changes without closing the window. If you choose **OK**, the changes will be accepted and the window will close. If you did this, reopen the **Date/Time** window with a double click.
- Now click on the tab for **Date & Time**.
- Is the month correct? If not, click on the ▼ down arrow to the right of the month. Find the correct month and click on it.
- Is the date correct? If not, click on the correct date.
- Is the hour correct? If not, move the mouse arrow onto the shown hour, then click and drag over the hour. It should be highlighted in blue. You can either type the correct hour using the number keys on your keyboard or use the ▲▼ arrows to the right of the time to increase or decrease the hour.
- Do the same for the minutes and seconds—highlight them and make the necessary changes.

• Once the correct hour, minute and second are visible on the screen, click on **OK**. The window should close, accepting your changes and putting you back in the Control Panel window.

Mouse Traps

Now we'll customize the mouse to suit you. If you prefer to have the mouse to your left, you can also reverse the functions of the mouse buttons here (see "Southpaws" box). Let's adjust the double-click speed.

• Double-click on the **Mouse** icon.

You may click on all the file tabs and read what each contains, but the ones we'll focus on are **Buttons** and **Motion**.

• Click on the **Buttons** tab to adjust the double-click timing.

• Look at the pointer that indicates how slow or fast the clicking is set. Do you naturally click slower or faster than where it is set at present? Click and drag the pointer in whichever direction makes sense for you.

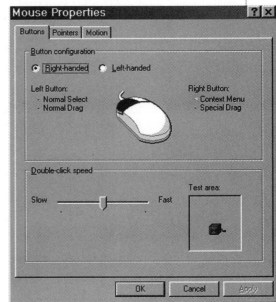

This window allows you to adjust your mouse settings.

• When you have found the right timing, move the mouse arrow to **Apply** and click once. (Remember, this means that your change has been accepted and the window will remain open.)

Now let's click on the **Motion** tab.

Here we're interested in the **Cursor Speed and Acceleration.** There is a pointer that indicates the speed with which the mouse arrow will move across the screen (the computer refers to the mouse arrow as a cursor here). Move the mouse arrow onto that pointer. Click and drag the pointer to the speed where you think it should be. Mine is set on the slowest speed, which is easiest for me, but by all means be the judge of what's best for you. You can always come back to this window and readjust it at a later date.

Once you've clicked on the word **OK**, your changes will be made and the window will close.

Hanging Wallpaper

The background on your desktop screen is also referred to as wallpaper. Your operating software offers several different styles of wallpaper.

Double-click on the **Display** window in your Control Panel. Here we can choose your wallpaper, change the look of the screen and create a screen saver.

The first tab available is **Background.** This is where you decide the background for the desktop screen. A mini computer screen on the window displays a sample of whichever wallpaper you click on. This screen may not be big enough for you to get a sense of what the wallpaper

looks like. Feel free to click on **OK**, then minimize the **Control Panel** window. This allows the wallpaper to be viewed in its actual size.

The Control Panel is now minimized on the Task Bar at the bottom of the screen. Click on the Control

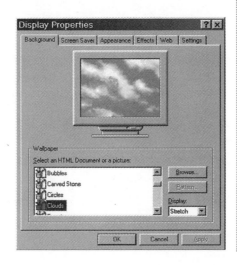

Reversing the Buttons

To reverse the tasks of your mouse's two buttons:

- Click on the arrow to the right of **Context Menu/Alternate Select**. Find **Click/Select** on the list (the Scroll Bar will have to be used to move the choices up). Click once on **Click/Select**.
- Now click on the arrow to the right of the **Click/Select** box that is at the top of the window (not the one you just changed). Find **Context Menu/Alternate Select**. Click once on that.

In the Display Properties window you can change the look of your screen's background.

What Am I Saving My Screen From?

Screen savers were originally designed to protect the screen from "screen burn." Computer screens used to become damaged when the same screen image remained on the screen for too long. Improvements in the design of screens make this unlikely. Nowadays screen savers are more for visual entertainment.

Display Properties also lets you choose a Screen Saver.

Panel box in the Task Bar to restore it to the screen. Move the mouse arrow to the **Display** icon and double-click to reopen it. Keep repeating this process until you find the wallpaper that suits you. You can select different wallpaper as often as you please.

While in the **Background** tab, let's decide one more thing about the way the desktop screen appears. Under the word **Display:** you have the option of **Tile, Center** or **Stretch,** which determines the appearance of the image on your screen. Click on the ▼ arrow to the right to expose these choices. Click on whichever you prefer. Again, if after it is viewed on the desktop screen you don't like it, you can always come back to Hanging Wallpaper and change it.

Now, click on the **Screen Saver** tab. A screen saver is an image that appears on the screen when the computer is on and has sat unused for a period of time. This tab allows you to decide what the screen saver will look like and when it will appear.

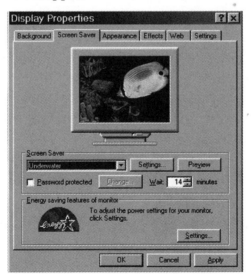

Under the words **Screen Saver** there is a box with an ▼ arrow to the right. Click on the arrow to expose the screen saver options. You may have to use the Scroll Bar to see everything that is available. Click on the screen saver you want to see displayed and then click on **OK**.

Click on **Settings** to see the options available to customize your choice. Some screen savers offer a choice of colors or images.

Click on **Preview** to see your screen saver choice displayed in its actual size without having to close the window. Move the mouse arrow to get back to the **Display** window.

The last decision that you need to make is how much time should elapse before the screen saver is activated. Do this by changing the number next to the word **Wait:**. Click on the ⬆⬇ up and down arrows to the right of the number. Once you have decided on the length of time (I have mine set at 10 minutes), click on **OK**. Your changes have been made and the window will be closed. Close the **Control Panel** window. Now you're back at the desktop screen.

This might be a fine time to take a break. Just leave your computer as it is and come back when you're ready. When you return, we'll go over some more features.

Screen Saver Password

If the **Screen Saver** tab gives you the option to choose a password, my recommendation is don't. Passwords need to be remembered. A screen saver just doesn't warrant a password.

The Task Bar

The **Task Bar** is the gray bar at the bottom of your screen. It offers an alternative way to access application software programs and other areas of the computer.

The computer usually offers more than one way to skin a cat. By that I mean that there is usually more than one way to accomplish a task or complete an action on the computer.

The Task Bar.

Move the mouse arrow onto the time in the right hand corner of the Task Bar and click the *right* mouse button. Now move the arrow to **Adjust Date/Time** and click once with the *left* mouse button. You've opened the **Date/Time Properties** window that we accessed from the Control Panel. All the same date and time changes that we made before can be done by opening the window this way.

Close the **Date/Time** window. (Remember, use the ⊠ Close Box.) Now with the mouse arrow on a blank spot on the desktop screen, click once with the *right* mouse button. Move the arrow to the word **Properties** and click once with the *left* mouse button. It's the **Display Properties** window that we used to pick your wallpaper and screen saver.

Experiment with what happens when the left or right button is clicked on an item. You can open all the icons on the desktop screen and see what they contain. For that matter, you can click on anything on the computer screen as long as you don't press the **Enter** key, which instructs the computer to take an action, or you don't click on an action key (**OK, Yes, Apply** . . .). If you open a window and are concerned that you're heading into unknown territory, simply close it by using the ⊠ Close Box or click on the word **Cancel, Finish** or **Exit** or click on a blank area of the screen.

Getting in the Swing

It's a lovely thing to listen to music while working (or playing) at the computer. Grab a CD that you enjoy, and we'll learn how to play music.

- Open the D: drive on your computer case by pressing the button near the drive.

The D: drive is where you insert a CD-ROM.

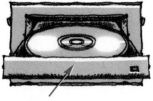

D: DRIVE

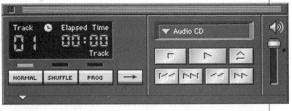

The window that will appear when you put in an audio CD looks something like this. It allows you to choose a CD track and adjust the volume.

- Place the CD, label side up, on the CD tray and press the button again to close the tray. *You don't ever want to force the tray closed by pushing the tray in—it is a very delicate component of the computer.*

• A window will appear on the screen with options for the track you want to play and what volume you prefer. Here you will use the mouse to choose your options. For example, move the mouse onto the volume arrow. Click and drag the arrow either up or down to increase or decrease the volume.

• After you've set your preferences, click on the ▬ Minimize Box. To maximize the window, click once on the box that contains the minimized window in the Task Bar.

You can also access the D: drive through the **My Computer** icon. Double-click on My Computer, then double-click on **Control Panel**. The D: drive is accessed by double-clicking on the D: icon.

There are a couple of other options for controlling the volume. If your computer came with speakers, they may have controls, or your monitor may have a volume control. Fiddle around to set a comfortable volume for you. The other place where the volume can be adjusted is the little horn 🔊 on the right side of the Task Bar near where the actual time is displayed. Left-click on the symbol and a window will appear where you can control the CD's volume.

When the CD has stopped (either by your choice or because it came to an end), simply press the button near the D: drive on your computer case to "eject" the CD. Remove the CD and press the button again to close the drive.

Job Well Done

If you've been using this book sequentially, at this point you should see a light at the end of the tunnel. The computer is more and more under your control. Stick with the book, and by the end you'll be in total control. You can repeat any part of this chapter and the previous one until you are ready to go on the Internet in Chapter 13.

Learning the ABCs

Each computer can vary slightly. In my experience there have been some computers that refer to the drive for the CD-ROM as the E: drive instead of the D: drive. The literature that came with your machine will clarify if your CD-ROM drive is referred to as D: or E:.

Welcome, Mac Users

When you open an icon or folder, it's important that the arrow is placed on the icon and not on the text description below the icon.

Turn on your computer. In this chapter we will customize some features on your computer and investigate a few others. Feel free to move at your own pace. You can stop and start wherever and whenever you want.

Let's investigate what the desktop screen has to offer. First, move the mouse arrow onto the Apple logo in the top left corner of the screen and click once. A box with a lot of options will have opened. Move the mouse arrow onto the words **Control Panels** and click once. If the box didn't stay open, click on the Apple logo again but hold the mouse button down and move the mouse arrow onto the Control Panels, and release the button. The Control Panels window will open. If it didn't, give it another try. I want you to see the icons on your screen, not just in this illustration.

If your Control Panel window looks different from the illustration, we need to change it to appear with icons.

Move the mouse arrow up to the word **View** and hold down the mouse button. Move down to the words **as Icons** and release the mouse. A ✓ should appear to the left. A check indicates which choice is active.

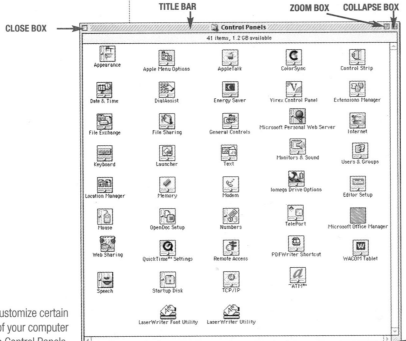

You can customize certain parts of your computer using the Control Panels.

Later you can use View to change any window to the format you prefer.

What's in the Window?

Notice that the Control Panels window has the same features as the **untitled folder** window. It has a **Title Bar**, ☐ **Close Box**, ⬛ **Zoom Box**, ⬛ **Collapse Box** and a ◪ **Size Box**. What we haven't discussed yet on this window is the **Scroll Bar** on the bottom and the right side of the window. The Scroll Bar will always appear on an open window, but it isn't active unless the arrows ▼, ▲, ◀, ▶ are in black, not gray.

The size of the window dictates how much of the information in the window you will be able to see. This is when the Scroll Bar comes in handy. The Scroll Bar allows you to move the information in the window up and down for full viewing.

An active Scroll Bar (with black, not gray, arrows) indicates that the window has more to offer than what's on your screen. You can increase the size of the window or scroll the window to see what else it contains. Students often call me because they can't find an item that they know is in a certain window. Usually it is right where it should be, but they didn't see all the contents of the window. An active Scroll Bar (arrows in black) is your clue that there is more to be unveiled. We'll experiment with this shortly.

Enlarging the Window The most efficient way to see all the contents of a window is to increase its size. You can do that in two ways. Once you have seen how each choice works, follow the instructions in italics to restore the window to its original form and go to the next option. We will experiment with scrolling after you have tried the following options.

Option 1. There is a box in the Title Bar that will increase the size of the window. Do you remember which box that is?

Experiment

As I describe some of the many icons contained in the **Control Panels** window, feel free to double-click on the icon to open it and see what's inside. To get back to the Control Panels window, close the window you've opened. (Remember the ☐ Close Box?) If somehow you have closed the Control Panels window, move the mouse onto the Apple logo and down to the words Control Panels and click once.

Click and Drag . . . Is It a Drag?

Are you having some trouble with the click and drag maneuver? Let's review:

- Place the mouse arrow on the object you want to move and depress the mouse button.
- Keep the mouse button depressed while you drag the object (by moving the mouse) to where you desire.
- Take your finger off the mouse and the object will remain where it has been moved.

My advice is, *if you have Solitaire, keep playing. If not, keep playing with the jigsaw puzzle*. It may seem silly (or drive you nuts), but it is the best way to master the mouse. If you haven't been faithfully doing your homework, start today!

The ⊡ Zoom Box. Move the mouse arrow into the ⊡ Zoom Box and click once. (As I said in Chapter 11, sometimes the window thinks it is maximized, but it isn't taking up the entire screen. In that case the window can be maximized by using the ⊡ Size Box as described in Option 2.) *To restore, place the mouse arrow on the Zoom Box and click.*

Option 2. Move the mouse arrow to the ⊡ Size Box at the bottom right corner of the Control Panels window. As you did with the untitled folder window, click and drag the bottom right mouse arrow to the bottom right of the screen, then release the mouse button. *To restore, place the mouse arrow in the bottom right corner of the window. Click and drag the corner to the left and up until the window is the size it was when you first opened it.*

Scrolling Along

Sometimes there can be more icons contained in a window than can be seen no matter how large you make the window. In this case, you will have to use the Scroll Bar to see all that is available. The Scroll Bar is similar to an elevator: a button is pressed to activate it, it moves up and down and you can get off anyplace you want.

Does your window look like the window in the illustration on the facing page? Make sure that the Scroll Bar on the right side of the window is active. If the Scroll Bar isn't active, move the mouse arrow onto the lower right corner of your window. Click and drag the corner up and to the left until the arrows are black, indicating the Scroll Bar is active.

There should be a set of arrows at the top and bottom of the Scroll Bar positioned on the right edge of the window. The Scroll Bar also has a set of arrows on the bottom of the window positioned at the right and left. On some Macs the up and down arrows are next to each other. Let's take a scroll . . .

- Place the mouse arrow on the bottom ▼ scroll arrow on the right edge of the window and click a few times. With each click the screen moves down. *Be careful that the mouse arrow stays within the box that contains the scroll arrow. If your mouse wanders, you will not be able to activate the Scroll Bar, or the window may scroll in increments greater than you desire.*

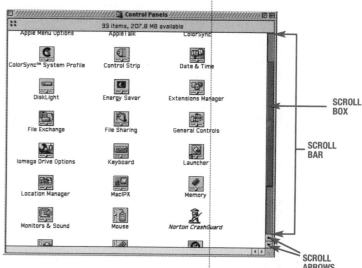

- The image within the window will move up if you place the mouse arrow on the top ▲ scroll arrow and click.

- The window will scroll left or right with the bottom ◀ left and ▶ right scroll arrows.

- If you hold down the mouse button rather than depressing and releasing it, the window will scroll very quickly. This technique is more difficult to control, but faster than individual clicks.

- You can also move what's in the window by placing the mouse arrow on the **Scroll Box** within the Scroll Bar and clicking and dragging the Scroll Box up or down. This is faster than using the scroll arrows and is most convenient if you're in a very large document wanting to get from, for example, page 1 to page 40.

Scroll Bars play a big role in web sites on the Internet. I strongly recommend that you spend time maneuvering a Scroll Bar every time you play on the computer until you have the technique down.

Does Anybody Really Know What Time It Is?

We're going to check to be sure that the date and time are set properly on your computer. Open the **Date & Time** window by double-clicking on the icon found on the Control Panels window. (You get the Control Panels

The appearance of a Scroll Bar indicates that you're not seeing all of the window's contents. Mastering the Scroll Bar is critical when you're on the Internet.

An Active Scroll Bar

It is a subtle difference, but when the Scroll Bar is active, the arrows at either end of the bar are black. When it is inactive, they are a light shade of gray.

window by clicking on the **Apple** ⬤ in the top left of your screen.) If you can't see the Date & Time icon, use the Scroll Bar to reveal it. To review double-clicking, place the mouse arrow on the icon again and depress, release, depress, release the mouse button in as rapid succession as you can. Think knock, knock. Keep trying, and eventually you will find the right timing.

Click on the **Set Time Zone** box. At the bottom of the window there are two buttons: **OK** and **Cancel**. These are your action choices. Sometimes a window will offer you **Help, Yes** or **No** as choices. When you click on any of these buttons, you're instructing the computer to take that action. You must be *very sure* of the action you want to take—sometimes it is irreversible.

Notice that the box containing **OK** has a slightly darker outline. In this case the computer assumes **OK** to be the most likely choice for you. Be forewarned, if you depress the **Return** key on your keyboard, whatever action the computer has selected will be taken. *This is why it is so important not to arbitrarily depress the **Return** key; you may unwittingly take an action that cannot be reversed.* (Note: It may not be OK that the computer preselects for you. It will be any action button that the computer deems will be your likely choice.) In the case of what we are playing with here, not to worry—nothing is irreversible.

Follow the steps below to adjust the **Time Zone**:

• Scroll to the city nearest where you live and click once.

Date & Time

Current Date

4/21/00

Date Formats...

Current Time

11:01:17 AM

Time Formats...

Time Zone

☐ Set Daylight-Saving Time Automatically
☐ Daylight-Saving Time is in effect

The time zone has not been specified.

Set Time Zone...

☐ **Use a Network Time Server**

Time server: Apple Americas/...

Clock has not been synchronized.

Server Options...

Menu Bar Clock

◉ On ○ Off

Clock Options...

This window allows you to set the date and time.

- Click on **OK** to accept that city to represent your time zone.

- Move the arrow to the ☐ box preceding **Daylight Savings Time**. Click on the box. A ✓ will appear in the box indicating that the choice is active.

Follow the steps below to adjust the **Current date**:

- If the month is not correct, move the mouse arrow onto the month and click. Hit the number on your keyboard for the correct month or use the ▭ arrows.

- If the day is not correct, click on the day and do the same as above.

- If the year is not correct, click on the year and do the same again.

Follow the steps below to adjust the **Current Time** section of the window.

- Click on the **Time Formats** box.

- Move the mouse arrow and click on either the ◯ 12-hour or the ◯ 24-hour button. It's always a struggle for me to decipher military time (24-hour), but it's available if you prefer that.

- Move the mouse arrow in to the **Noon & midnight** area and click on ◯ 12:00.

- Click on **OK** to accept these choices.

- Now that you are back in the **Date & Time** window, is the hour correct in the **Current Time** box? If not, move the mouse onto the hour and click. Hit the number on your keyboard for the correct hour or use the ▭ arrows.

- Do the same for the minutes and seconds.

- Click on **AM** or **PM**. Hit the **A** or **P** key on the keyboard to change it to the correct choice.

- Click on an empty gray area of the **Date & Time** window to have the clock begin keeping time.

- Move the arrow to the ▭ Close Box and click to close the window.

Mouse Traps

Now we'll customize the mouse to suit you. Double-click on the **Mouse** icon.

Mouse Tracking has ◯ buttons indicating the speed of the mouse arrow. Click on the ◯ button that represents how fast you would like the mouse to move.

Mine is set on the slowest speed, which is easiest for me, but by all means you be the judge of what's best for you. You can always come back to this window and readjust it at a later date.

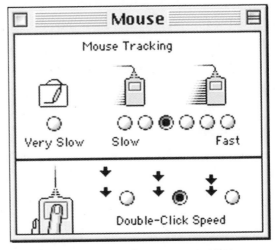

This window allows you to adjust your mouse settings.

There is also a choice about the timing of the double click. Click on whichever button best represents how you double-click. I double-click very quickly. This, too, can be changed easily if you need the timing adjusted.

A **Mouse Track** is a kind of shadow that follows the mouse arrow as it moves on the screen. On your system you may not have this feature or the option to adjust it. Mine does and I opt not to have it appear, but if you want it, click on either **Short** or **Long**.

You may also have the option of having a thick or thin I-beam cursor. The I-beam appears when the mouse is in a text area. This choice is also subjective. You can always come back to this window and change these preferences whenever you wish. Once the **Mouse** window is closed, your changes will be made.

This is a fine time to take a break. Just leave your computer as it is and come back when you're ready. When you return, we'll go over some more features.

Selecting a Background

Here we will change the look of the background for the desktop screen and create a screen saver.

• Is the Control Panels window still open on your screen? If not, go to the ● Apple logo and access the Control Panels (look on page 152 for how to open the Control Panels). Find the **Desktop Patterns** icon. (If your Mac has OS 8, look for the **Desktop Pictures** icon.) Double-click on the icon to see its contents.

• Click on the **Pattern** box.

• Scroll using the arrows at the bottom of the image to see what other patterns are available.

• When you find a pattern you like, move the mouse arrow to the **Set Desktop** (or **Set Desktop Pattern**) box and click once.

• If the pattern does not appear on the screen, it might be covered by a photograph. Either click on **Remove Picture** or click on **Picture Box**, then **Remove Picture**. Bingo! There's your pattern.

If you would prefer a picture to a pattern for the background of your desktop screen (not all systems offer this), follow the steps below.

• Click on the **Picture** box.

• If you have a **Show Preview** box, move the mouse arrow into the □ **Show Preview** box and click. A ✓ should appear in the box to indicate that you want to preview the picture choice.

• Otherwise, click on the **Select Picture** box. This should open a box containing the words **Sample Picture Files** or **Sample Desktop Pictures**. (If the **Sample Picture Files**

In the Desktop Patterns window, you can change the look of your screen's background.

did not open, go to the instructions below. It is more involved to find that folder, but we can do it!)

• Click on each of the pictures offered to see which you prefer. When you've found the picture you like most, move the mouse arrow to **OK** or **Open** and click once.

• Now click on the **Set Desktop** button.

• The last decision to make is how the picture will be positioned on the screen. There is a dialog box that offers **Tile on Screen, Center on Screen, Scale to Screen, Fill Screen** or **Position Automatically**. Click on the arrows to the right to reveal all the options.

• Click on whichever pleases you. A ✓ check will appear to confirm your choice. Now click **Set Desktop.**

All of these decisions can be changed as often as you desire. You will need to click on **Remove Picture** before you can set a new picture in its place. Otherwise, follow the steps above to make any changes.

If **Sample Picture Files** didn't appear when you clicked on **Select Picture**, here's what needs to happen.

• Move the mouse arrow to the Apple logo at the top left of the screen and click.

• Move down to **Find File** and click once.

• Type the words **Sample Desktop**, then click on the word **Find**. (It must be "on all disks.")

• Move the mouse arrow onto **Sample Desktop Pictures** and double-click.

• If a **Photos** folder appears, you'll need to double-click on that folder.

• Also close the **Items Found, Find File** and the **Control Panels** windows.

• You must click and drag whatever image you want to see onto the preview monitor.

• When you've settled on an image, click on the **Set Desktop** button. If you have a choice of **Don't Set, Cancel** or **Set** as your actions, click on **Set**.

You can open all the items in the Control Panels and see what they contain. For that matter, you can click on anything on the computer screen as long as you don't hit the **Return** key, which instructs the computer to take an action, or don't click on an action key (**OK, Yes, Apply**). If you open a window and are concerned that you're heading into unknown territory, simply close it by using the ☐ Close Box or click on the word **Cancel, Finish** or **Exit**.

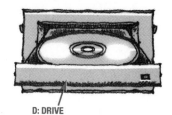

D: DRIVE

The D: drive is where you insert a CD-ROM.

Getting in the Swing

It's a lovely thing to listen to music while working (or playing) at the computer. Grab a CD that you enjoy, and we'll learn how to play music.

• Open the D: drive on your computer case by pressing the button near the drive.

• Place the CD, label side up, on the CD tray and press the button again to close the tray. *You don't ever want to force the tray closed by pushing it in yourself—it is a very delicate component of the computer.*

• The music may start playing as soon as you close the CD tray.

• Move the mouse arrow to the Apple logo and click. Now move it down to **Apple CD Audio Player** and click once. If you can't find it there, move the mouse arrow to the Apple logo and click **Control Panels**; press down the mouse button and don't release it until you have landed on **Apple CD Audio Player.** If you don't have the **Apple CD Audio Player** in the Control Panels, double-click on the icon that looks like a CD on your desktop screen.

• A window will appear where you can set the volume and select the track

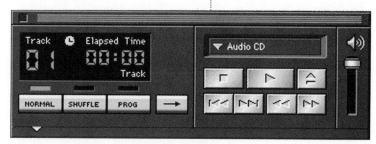

When you insert an audio CD, the window that will appear looks something like this. It allows you to choose a CD track and adjust the volume.

you want to listen to. Close this window after you have made your selections.

To eject the CD-ROM , on a MAC, click and drag the icon into the Trash.

There are a couple of other options for controlling the volume. Your speakers or monitor may have a volume control. Fiddle with them to set a comfortable volume for you.

When you want to remove the CD, simply click and drag the CD icon into the 🗑 **Trash** on the desktop. If that doesn't expel the CD, you might have to press the button by the D: drive. Remove the CD and press the button again to close the drive.

Job Well Done

If you've been using the book sequentially, at this point you should see a light at the end of the tunnel. The computer is more and more under your control. Stick with the book, and by the end you'll be in total control. Repeat any part of this chapter and the previous one until you are ready to go on the Internet in Chapter 13.

In This Case Trash 🗑 Is Not Gone Forever

Normally when you drag something into the Trash, you're throwing it away. In the case of a floppy disk or a CD, you are simply instructing the computer to eject the disk.

The
Newlywed
Game

13

Spanning the Globe
"Surfing the net"— traveling around the World Wide Web

The Internet looms in front of us as the Wild West did for the early settlers. As we hear more about the Internet and its limitless possibilities, none of us wants to be left behind. It is the land of opportunity, yet it is full of unknowns and it may seem like a long, hard journey to get there. Take heart, it is not uncharted ground. We will access the Internet and learn about web sites together.

If you are chomping at the bit to get to e-mail, you can move on to the next chapter and come back to this chapter later. However, I strongly suggest that you go through this chapter first, as it has information that will inform your e-mail experience.

An Overview

The Internet is a huge system that connects computers all over the world by telephone lines. The World Wide Web is today's modernization of the old government-issue Internet, which consisted of convoluted codes on a black screen. The World Wide Web (www) was designed to make the Internet accessible, with colorful graphics, sound and a user-friendly environment.

Who Created the Internet?

In the 1960s, the U.S. government feared its computers would become targets for foreign enemies. To prevent that from happening, it devised a technology to transfer information from one computer to another by way of telephone lines. This would ensure that information was in several different places so there would be no single target. This was the precursor to the Internet as we know it.

Surfing the net (net = Internet) isn't very different from channel-hopping on your television set. Sometimes something will really hold your interest; other times it's fun to change from one image to the next; and then there are times when everything seems just plain awful. The Internet, like TV, can be seductive, a great way to escape and an opportunity to learn something new. All you need to connect to the Internet is a computer, a modem, a phone line and an Internet service provider or online service to provide access to the Internet.

Finding Your Online Service

When you've registered with an online service, you have the benefit of the services that it has put together for you. Your service will have chosen from the web certain periodicals, travel resources, shopping areas and much more, and will have direct links to them for your convenience. Each online service varies with what it offers. All of them provide access to the Internet and e-mail. When you buy your computer, one or several online services will have arranged to have their software preinstalled on the hard drive.

If you want an online service other than your preinstalled choices, you can look under "Computer Online Services" in the Yellow Pages. Most services offer a free trial period. Remember, in choosing a service you want to be sure that they have a local access number in your area or you will incur long-distance charges while you surf the net.

The process of registering with an online service is another one of those cases where you might want to call in the cavalry. Ask a friend or relative to come over and help you get started.

Proud PC Owners

You will most likely have a choice among Microsoft Network, America Online, CompuServe, Prodigy and AT&T as your online service. The icons for these services may be on your desktop screen. If not, look for the folder labeled **Online Services** and double-click on the folder. If there is no folder, move the mouse arrow to **Start** and click, then move up to **Programs** and across to **Online Services**. A small box will appear containing your online service options.

Proud Mac Owners

America Online or Earthlink are the online services that will probably be preinstalled on your hard drive. If their icons aren't on your desktop screen, access them by moving the mouse arrow onto your 🖴 Hard Disk icon and double-clicking. If that window doesn't reveal the icon, open your **Applications** window with a double click to look for their icons. Remember to use the Scroll Bar to see *all* the contents of the window.

Customer Service

Pay very careful attention if a customer service number appears on the screen at any time and be sure to write it down. After you've completed the registration process, that number can be rather elusive. This may be your only opportunity to note the number. Grab it while you can.

Registering Your Account

You should have a credit card, paper and a writing utensil ready before registering with your online service. Double-click the icon of whichever online service you've chosen. Follow the instructions that appear on the screen for both installation and setup. The process of registering with an online service can take some time. It may involve installing software and restarting your computer.

A Reminder to Keep Track of Your Trial Subscription

Many online services offer a free trial period. It is very important that you remember to cancel your trial subscription if you no longer want the service. Even though you won't be billed for the trial period, the online service provider will have asked for your credit card information to start your account. If you forget to cancel the account, it will start billing your credit card when the trial period is over and continue to do so until you cancel the subscription. Mark your calendar—there will be no reminder from the online service provider.

Sometimes when you install application software, you will be instructed to restart your computer. This is to ensure that the information from the software has been properly stored in the hard drive.

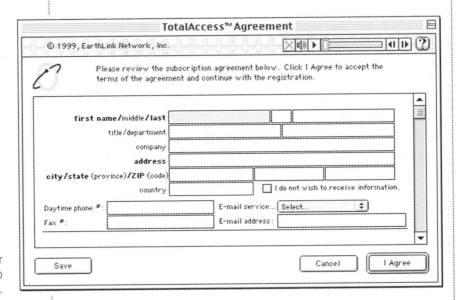

When you sign up with your online service, you'll have to register your account.

You'll be asked to type in your name, address, phone number and credit card information so that your online service can bill you monthly. Generally, you can move from one text box to another by hitting the **Tab** key (located to the left of Q on the keyboard). If you want to access a text box out of sequence, you can move the mouse arrow anywhere inside the white part of the text box and click to activate the text box. You'll see a flashing vertical line (referred to as the cursor or blinking cursor) in the far left of the box. That indicates that you can start typing at that location. (Refer to Chapter 12 if you need a refresher on how to use the Scroll Bar.)

Don't Forget to Click in the Box!

This is a crucial thing to remember. It is the most common thing that people forget. *You must click inside the text box to activate it so it will accept your typing instructions.*

Choosing a User Name and Password

A user name is the name you use when you're on the Internet or sending e-mail. Example: If I were an America Online customer, and my user name was Peach, my e-mail address would be peach@aol.com. Even if you plan only to surf the net and never intend to send an e-mail, you will have to establish a user name and password. Your user name and password are how your online service identifies you. You don't need to use your name in your e-mail address. In fact, many people opt not to because they want to keep some anonymity.

Now that I've mentioned it, let's identify all the parts of my fictitious e-mail address.

peach@aol.com is the e-mail address.
peach is the user name.
@ means "at."
aol.com is the "domain name," or mailing address.

"Case sensitivity" means that it matters whether the letters are in upper or lower case. At this time most online services are *not* case sensitive when dealing with user names. Having said that, I still try to type my user name in the same case that I originally chose. Because passwords can be case sensitive, it is important that your password be typed in the same case as you originally chose. For this reason it is easier to choose a password that is all in lower case.

When deciding on your user name, keep in mind that people will need to know your e-mail address so that they can send you e-mail. It seems silly to point that out, but I've had clients pick rather embarrassing user names and regret it when they had to tell people, "My e-mail address is iamanidiot@msn.com." Your e-mail address shouldn't be

Everything Is in Caps. Why?

Beware. Above the **Shift** key is the **Caps Lock** key. If your finger accidentally depresses **Caps Lock**, you will need to depress it again to deactivate it. *Example:* I HIT THE CAPS LOCK KEY AND EVERYTHING IS IN UPPERCASE. i just hit it again and every- thing is in lower case.

hard to remember, such as al754blu1@compuserve.com. That name may mean something to you, but it's a nightmare to type and remember, particularly for others who might want to communicate with you.

Be prepared not to get the user name that you hoped for. With millions of people on the Internet, it's probable that someone may already have your first choice of user name. Have several options ready.

The online service will also ask for a password. A password verifies who you are each time you sign on to the service. Choose a password that comes easily to you. There isn't a whole lot of espionage with home computers, so you needn't come up with something really far out. But *please* don't use the same password that you use for your bank account or ATM card.

Make sure you write down your e-mail address and password. For safe keeping, why not stash it in your "Computer Instructions" envelope?

Once you've successfully registered, I want you to sign off and sign on from scratch. Practice, practice, practice.

Signing Off and Signing On

Each online service has its own quirks and requirements when you sign on. Some remember your user name and password, and others ask that the information be typed in every time. If you need to type information into a text box, remember to click on the box with your mouse to activate the text box and use **Tab** to get from one text box to the next.

What is that squeaking and squealing? You may hear the sound of the modem calling the online service. Find the volume control and adjust it, but remember to turn the

Action Buttons

Notice that one of the action buttons is usually either framed in a darker box or surrounded by dots. As discussed in Chapter 12, the computer is presuming that this is the action you will take. You can take this action by either hitting **Enter**, **Return** or moving the mouse arrow on the action key you want and clicking once.

volume back up when you get online because some web sites have sounds that you won't want to miss.

Each online service also has its own way of signing off. For some it is simply clicking on the Close Box. For others you need to maximize their box in the Task Bar and then click on **Disconnect.** There will be a tutorial or a tour offered that will help you discover the ins and outs of your particular service.

Error Messages, Busy Signals and Getting Cut Off

You may have heard people complain about how long it takes for them to sign on to their online service. There was a big hullabaloo a couple years ago about AOL (America Online) having tremendous wait times. It can happen to any online service. The phone lines are overburdened and the technology is so new that they're still inventing it as they go along. AOL was affected because of the number of people who signed on. They simply weren't equipped to handle the volume of new members. If you have trouble, try getting online at off hours. I use the Internet very early in the morning and late at night and rarely have any problems signing on.

An error message may appear when you are trying to sign on. Read it carefully. It could be telling you something as simple as your phone line isn't plugged into your modem or that it got a busy signal. At any rate, don't hesitate to call for technical help. Technical support is offered by every online service, so take advantage of it. If you have only one phone line, the technician will have to describe the solution. He or she won't be able to walk you through the problem while you're signed on because you'll be calling from the

Security on the Internet

There are scoundrels wherever you go who try to scam somebody out of something. The Internet is no different— no better and no worse. If you're comfortable buying things by mail order, you should be comfortable buying things on the Internet. You *will have* to give your credit card number to your online service to get connected, but if it makes you nervous you might not want to shop on the web.

same phone line that your computer uses when you're connected to the Internet. In this case it is especially important to write down exactly what appeared on the screen so you can tell the technician.

There are times when an error message might appear and it will have nothing to do with anything that you've done. Be patient and try what you were doing again. Even try signing off and on again. Sometimes the computer gets a false start and needs a second try.

Getting cut off while online is not an uncommon occurrence. It can happen because of an incoming call or perhaps because you've been online for a while but have been idle. Online services don't want their members to be signed on but not actually active (perhaps taking a break) because it slows down their transmissions. So if you're signed on but not using the service for a time, they may opt to sign you off.

Your Start Page

The first page that appears for your online service is the Start Page. These are as individual as the cover of a book. Each online service is constantly updating and modifying the look of their web pages.

Slowly move the mouse arrow around the Start Page. Do you notice that over certain words the arrow becomes a hand? Whenever the hand appears, you are being notified that there is an item that can be clicked on that will link you to more information on that topic. Generally, a single click will open the item.

Feel free to open *any* and *all* areas of the Start Page. You can't get into any trouble. If you don't like what you see, simply close the window, or back out of the window by clicking on the Back icon at the top left of the screen.

A Real Page-Turner

Start Page = the first page of your online service

Home Page = the first page of any web site on the Internet

Web Page = any page that follows the home page of a web site

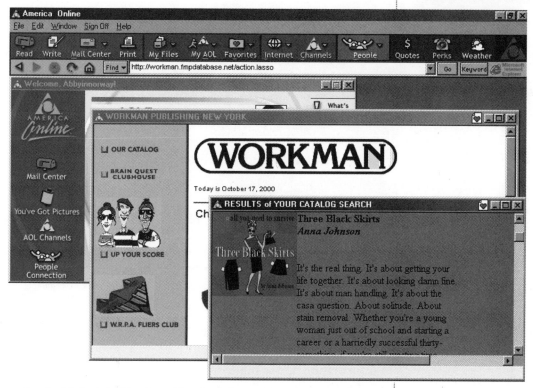

From back to front, the Start Page of America Online, the Home Page of my publisher's web site, a web page on the same web site.

Youth Safety While Online

There is a lot of very justified concern about how to keep children safe when they access the Internet. If you're going to invite your grandchildren to use your computer, please sit them down and explain the dangers of meeting someone over the Internet. They should NEVER give anyone their full name, home address or phone number.

Call the National Center for Missing and Exploited Children (800-843-5678) to receive the brochure "Child Safety on the Information Highway."

Maximize

Remember to maximize your window whenever possible. It makes reading things on the Internet much easier and much more pleasant (refer to Chapter 11).

66 *One night I couldn't sign on to the Internet and none of the people I usually rely on for computer guidance were around. So I had no choice but to call for technical help. It wasn't fun and it took almost an hour. But we fixed the problem. I wouldn't ask for it to happen again, but if it does, I know I can handle it.* **99**
—Evelyn

● *Advertisements*

Most online services allow advertisements to pop up. Usually they appear when you first sign on. You do *not* want to approve any purchase by accident, but don't worry because this isn't an easy thing to do. Don't click on any action button (**Yes, OK, Apply**, etc.) or hit the **Enter** or **Return** keys casually. I never even read these ads. I simply close the window or click on whatever action button indicates that I am not interested (**No, Exit, Close** etc.).

Web Sites and Their Addresses

Your online service is the launchpad to the web. Before we venture out to cyberspace, let's review some basic elements of all web sites. A web site is much like a book. It's full of information and is made up of pages. The pages of a web site are called web pages. The first page on a web site is called the Home Page.

There are several different parts to a web address. Each part gives the Internet information about how to locate the web site you're seeking. Don't confuse a web site address with an e-mail address. A web site starts with www. and doesn't have the @ symbol. Here is what an e-mail address looks like:

peach@aol.com

Here is what the average web address looks like:

http://www.abbyandme.com

Now let's define the parts:

http:// is the hypertext transfer protocol. AAAAaaaarrrrgggghhh! The good thing is that you don't need to know what that means. You don't even have to type it when you're inputting a web address.

www. stands for World Wide Web. Notice there is a period after www. Some web sites don't require that you type www., but I suggest that you do until none of the web sites require it (so there is no confusion). You need to be very careful about typing the address exactly as it appears; a spelling or punctuation change can send you to a different web site. It's just as if you dialed a wrong number on the phone. There will *never* be a space in a web site because that breaks the line of communication.

abbyandme. is the domain name, not unlike the user name in your e-mail address. If you wanted to create a web site, you would start by purchasing a domain name.

com is another part of the domain name. This extension gives you a clue to the type of web site. In this case, "com" indicates that it is a commercial web site. Note that it is *not* followed by a period. Here are the most common domain name extensions:

.com = commercial	.nom = personal
.edu = educational	.firm = company
.gov = government	.arts = arts and culture
.mil = military	.rec = recreational
.org = organization	.store = place to shop
.net = network business	.info = information

So take a stab at what the web site might be for 1600 Pennsylvania Avenue, Washington, D.C. You guessed it! www.whitehouse.gov

Look Out, Web, Here We Come

It's time to surf the net.

At the top of the online service's Start Page there is a long text box. It may or may not already have text in it. No matter. Move the mouse arrow anywhere inside the box

Surfing the Net vs. Surfing the Web

They are one and the same. And when you're doing either, you're on the information superhighway.

and click once. If there was text in the box, it is now highlighted probably in blue or yellow. This is where you will type in a web address. Remember, you don't need to type in http://.

• Move the mouse arrow into the text box on the Start Page and click once. When you start typing, the now-highlighted text will automatically be replaced with what you type.

• Type www.whitehouse.gov and hit **Enter** or **Return** or move the mouse and click on **GO**.

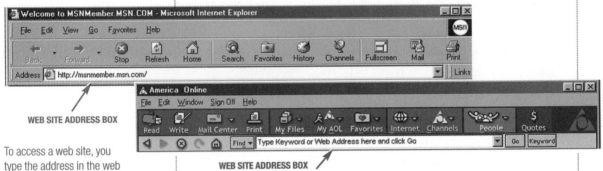

WEB SITE ADDRESS BOX

To access a web site, you type the address in the web site address box. Seen here are the web site address boxes for Microsoft Network and America Online.

WEB SITE ADDRESS BOX

Before your very eyes is the Home Page of the web site for the White House. If it hasn't appeared yet, be patient. A web site with a lot of graphics (pictures) can take quite a while to appear on the screen. If it's taking so long that you want to throw in the towel, click on the **Stop** or **X** on the

The Home Page of the White House's web site.

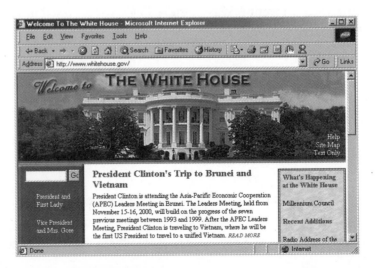

Tool Bar (not to be mistaken for the Close Box in the Title Bar).

Want to do something fun? Let's access my web site.

- Move the mouse arrow into the text box and click once.
- Type: **www.abbyandme.com** and hit **Enter** or **Return** or click on **GO**.

Welcome to my web site. Make yourself at home. Click on anything that tickles your fancy. I want you to feel that my web site is a safe and comfortable place for you to return to each time you connect to the Internet. It may be the only web site that you go to for a while. That is perfectly fine. Take your time to get acquainted with this site and all it has to offer. Before you know it, you'll be skillfully zooming around the Internet.

You'll notice that the information in **abbyandme.com** is constantly changing and being updated. Web sites need to be movable feasts or why would you go back for a second visit?

There is a list of web sites at the end of the book. Check them out and access any of the web addresses that interest you.

Moving Around a Web Site

Open up one of the web sites listed at the end of the book. Look carefully at the web site you opened. Notice that certain words may be in brighter colors or underlined. They are specifically designed that way to get your attention. Remember, when the mouse arrow becomes a hand, that indicates there is more to be found if you click on those words.

The words or images that you can click on are called links. They link you to more information or sometimes to another web site on the same topic. On my web site, you'll find that each page is designed to have links to specific categories (travel, finance, etc.). Once you've clicked on a link, you will be taken to a different web site. It just goes on and on and on. Play around with my web site or others as much as you want, then come back to the book.

A Gentle Touch

If you hold down a key on the keyboard, it will keep tttttttttttyping. Use a quick depress and release to hit the key you want without having it rrrrrrepeat.

Wanderlust

It may be your personality to meander along without a destination. This is usually not fulfilling on the Internet. Have a web site you want to visit or a topic you want to research in mind. Otherwise, you may feel that you spent a lot of time going nowhere.

Some web sites have so much text it can be dizzying. Take your time. Don't feel obliged to read everything. Also don't feel obliged to stick to a web site that doesn't appeal to you. That's what surfing the net is all about—riding the wave of your choice.

I Want to Come Back Again and Again

If there's a web site you'll want to visit often, you should bookmark it so that you won't have to type in the web address every time you want to go there. When you read a book and you want to return to a page to continue reading, you simply stick a bookmark in that page. The same is true on the Internet. Each online service has a slightly different way to bookmark a web site.

Click on "Favorites" or "Bookmarks" to save web site addresses for future visits.

AOL offers a **Favorites** folder that you click on. In most other cases, you will click on the **Bookmark** icon at the top of the window. This is where you'll click to revisit the web site of your choice. When you want to open a web site that you have bookmarked, you simply click on your **Favorites** or **Bookmark** icon to reveal the web sites you've stored. Then click on the web site you want to access, and your online service will take you directly there.

Huh? What Happened?

Strange things do happen. Sometimes after typing in a web address to access a web page, you might receive an error message. First, make sure you typed the web address correctly. If there isn't a mistake in the address, the error might have nothing to do with you. Perhaps the web site is under construction or being updated or the online service is experiencing difficulties. Give it another try or go somewhere else and come back and try later.

Search Engines: Seek and Ye Shall Find

A search engine is a web site that finds information for you on the Internet. Think of search engines as competing libraries, each with slightly different archives and filing systems. When I found the Jack Russell terrier doormat and the theater tickets for Mom, I used a search engine. There are many search engines available. Your online service probably offers one. Because each search engine has a different library, you may find different information on different search engines. See "Some Recommended Web Sites" at the back of the book for a list of different search engines.

To see a search engine in action, we're going to visit one of my favorites—Ask Jeeves.

• Move the mouse arrow inside the web site address box at the top of the screen and click once to activate the box.

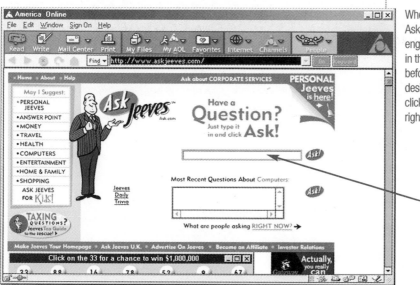

When using the Ask Jeeves search engine, you must click in the search text box before typing in your desired search. Then click on "Ask" to the right of the text box.

SEARCH TEXT BOX

• Type in www.askjeeves.com and hit **Enter** or **Return**, or click on **GO**.

• When the Ask Jeeves Home Page appears, click inside the search text box and type the word "waffles." Now move the mouse arrow to the word **Ask** and click.

Whichever search engine you use, these will be the basic steps. Each will have tips for you on how to conduct a search. Read and follow their suggestions.

Remember to use the Scroll Bar to view all of the results of your search. You will notice that to the right of some of the results there is an ▾ arrow. If you click on that arrow and hold down the mouse button, you'll see additional results. Move the mouse arrow onto any of the results that you want to see and click to highlight it. Move the mouse arrow onto the word **Ask** to the left of the result and click once. This will bring you to a web site that pertains to your search. If it isn't what you want, use the **Back** arrow (top left of the screen) to return to the original results of your search.

BACK ARROW

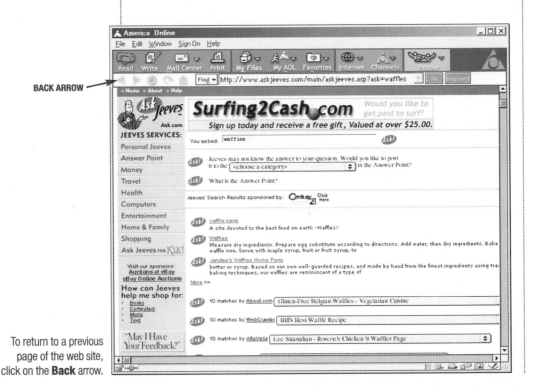

To return to a previous page of the web site, click on the **Back** arrow.

When you type in your search, be very specific. Search engines sort the results by the percentage of how it fulfills your search, but you may still find there's a lot to weed through. *Sometimes it helps to put the request in quotes. This instructs the search engine to look for web sites that contain all the words, not just one.* Each search engine also has categories listed on its Home Page. You might want to take a peek at these before you look further.

Print for Your Scrapbook

For those times when you want to have the information from a web site to read later or perhaps to pass on to someone else, you can always use your printer to print what appears on your computer screen.

You can either click on the **Printer** icon at the top of your screen or click on the word **File**, then move the mouse arrow down to the word **Print** and click. When the Printer window opens, hit **Enter** or **Return** or click on **Print** or **OK**. It's as simple as that. But don't be surprised if certain parts of the screen do not print out properly. That happens on some web sites and not on others.

If the page didn't print, check that the printer is turned on and plugged into the computer. You may have to click once on the web page that you want to print. Move the mouse arrow to a blank area on the web page and click. This signals the printer that this is the page you want to print, then go back and try to print again.

Chat Rooms

Your online service may offer chat rooms and/or forums. Refer to the introduction provided by your online service for how to access its chat rooms. These are places where people communicate live by sending typed messages back and forth about a given topic. Some of the chat rooms or forems are quite highbrow and informative. Some are pretty explicit and contain questionable subject matter. Be selective about where you go and how much information you choose to give about yourself. If you release your e-mail address, you may be inundated with e-mails from people you don't want to communicate with.

Never give someone your full name, home address or phone number. *Do not* give them any more personal information than you would a stranger on the telephone. Be aware that there are people lurking about in the recesses of the Internet hoping to find suckers to take advantage of. You are not a sucker and you are not about to become one!

A Chat Room Decoder

Here are some symbols and abbreviations that are used frequently, especially in chat rooms. (You can also entertain people by using them in your e-mails.)

:-)	smile	:´-(	crying
:)	also a smile	;-)	wink
:-D	laughing	:´-)	happy and crying
:-}	grin	:-@	screaming
:-(	frown	:-&	tongue-tied

BRB	be right back
BTW	by the way
FWIW	for what it's worth
GD&R	grinning, ducking and running
GMTA	great minds think alike
IMHO	in my humble opinion
LOL	laughing out loud
ROTFL	rolling on the floor laughing
TTFN	ta ta for now

What Did You Do Before the Internet?

I have no idea how you usually spend your time, but now and again you should sign off the Internet and do something else for a while. Seriously, a lot of time can pass while zooming around the web. Keep track of how long you're on. I set my kitchen timer for 40 minutes to make me aware of how long I have been online. Then I take a break, reset the timer, and continue my surfing. The point of the Internet is not to put you into a trance but to give you access to things you would otherwise not have available. Enjoy it, but don't let it take over your life.

■ HOMEWORK ASSIGNMENT

We will send e-mail in the next chapter, so ask your family and friends for their e-mail addresses.

14 Shall We Dance?
Let's send an e-mail

"Neither rain nor sleet nor gloom of night shall keep the carriers from their appointed rounds."

No matter how romantic all that seems, the antiquated form of mail delivery lives up to its new name . . . "snail mail." Not only does e-mail (electronic mail) arrive anywhere in the world within the blink of an eye, but you can also send as many e-mails as you want for the cost of a single local phone call. Pretty impressive.

An e-mail written by you to your daughter goes on quite a journey before it arrives on her computer screen, and amazingly it all happens in seconds.

You write the e-mail and send it to your daughter. Your online service routes the e-mail to a central brain for the Internet. That brain reads the e-mail address and routes it to your daughter's online service. Her online service holds the e-mail until she signs on. When your daughter signs on, any e-mail sent to her (including yours) will arrive in her mailbox. She then reads the e-mail, replies to you, and the cycle continues.

Again, recipients do not have to be home or have their computer on in order for you to send them e-mail. Their online service keeps it until they sign on.

If, indeed, you've chosen to skip over Chapter 13 and come straight here to send an e-mail, please be sure at some point to go back and read the previous chapter. It is full of helpful information for you to use while on the Internet.

"Letter writing had become a lost art form. I missed it. Now with e-mail I am writing more and loving it!"
—Alida

The E-mail Address

Your e-mail address is your user name (what you sign on with) plus the online service address. Example: If Brendan is my user name and MSN is the online service, then the e-mail address is Brendan@msn.com.

> **Brendan** is the user name.
>
> **@** means "at."
>
> **msn.com** is the domain name or mailing address.

When people recite their e-mail address to you, repeat it back to them. One error in letter, number or punctuation and your e-mail could be sent to someone else. Be sure not to type in Brendanatmsn.com. "At" is represented by holding down the Shift Key and depressing the 2 key— @ will then appear; "dot" is another way to say period.

Don't Forget to Click in the Box!

This is a crucial thing to remember. It is the most common thing that people forget. *You must click inside the text box to activate it so it will accept your typing instructions.*

Time to Send a Missive

Sign on to your online service. When the Start Page appears, move the mouse arrow to the Menu Bar at the top and click on the word **Mail**. If the Menu Bar doesn't offer **Mail**, look for an icon labeled **Mail** or **Write** and click on that. You should have options along the lines of **Read Mail** or **Get New Mail** and **Compose Mail** or **Create Mail**. Click on **Compose Mail**, **Create Mail**, **Write** or **New Message**. Each service is different but they will all have someplace to click to generate an e-mail template.

An e-mail form is now on your screen, ready and waiting to be filled in. It should look something like the templates on the following pages.

You're going to send your first e-mail to yourself. Again, each online service is slightly different, but here are the basic steps:

- There should be a flashing vertical line (referred to as the cursor or blinking cursor) in the left corner of the **To:** text box. If there isn't, move the mouse arrow into that box and click once.

- Type the recipient's e-mail address in the **To:** box. (In this case, because you are sending it to yourself, type in your e-mail address.) Look at it and be sure there are no mistakes. Hit **Tab** to move from box to box or click in the box with the mouse to activate it.

- Type something in the **Subject:** box, even if it is only "Hello." Some services won't let you send an e-mail without a subject. The purpose of the subject box is to help the recipient prioritize which e-mails to open first.

Generating an e-mail template is different, but straightforward, for each online service.

To:, Cc: and Bcc:

To: is where the recipient's e-mail address is typed.
Cc: stands for carbon copy. It means that this e-mail is being sent to another recipient.
Bcc: is a blind cc: The primary recipient won't know that you sent the e-mail to anyone else.

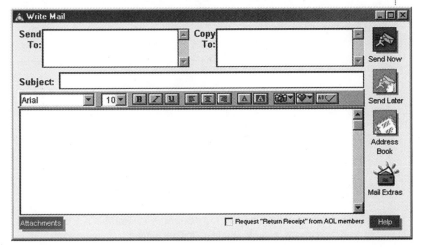

An America Online e-mail template. The recipient's e-mail address is typed in the "Send To:" box and your message is typed in the large text box below it.

Oops—I Made a Mistake

If you make a mistake, you can erase your typing (from right to left) by using the **BkSp** (Backspace) or **Delete** key. (Either can usually be found on the upper right section of your keyboard next to the + = key.) Depress it once for each letter that you want to erase. You'll see that it moves from right to left, deleting whatever precedes it on the screen. If you hold your finger down on the key, it will continue to move and delete to the left until you lift your finger up. You definitely have more control when you depress and release the key with each character than when you hold the key down.

• Now either move the mouse into the large text area and click or hit **Tab** again.

Before we type a message, I'll explain a couple of things. One of the big differences when you're typing on a computer as opposed to on a typewriter is that you don't need to hit **Enter** or **Return** at the end of a line. The text automatically moves, or wraps around, to the next line.

You do however need to use the **Return** or **Enter** key to create a new paragraph or to insert a blank line between text.

Now we get to type a message.

• Type in whatever you would like to say. Example: Mirror, mirror on the wall, who is playing with the computer and having a ball?

• When you're done, move the mouse arrow onto the word **Send** or **Send Now** and click once.

• Some online services ask that you acknowledge that the e-mail was sent. If this is the case, move the mouse arrow onto the word **OK** and click.

And away it goes!

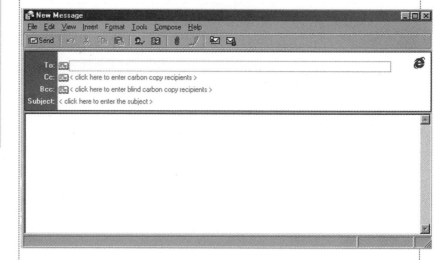

A Microsoft Network e-mail template. The recipient's e-mail address is typed in the "To:" box and your message is typed in the large text box below it.

You've Got Mail!

If the service is very busy, it might take a few minutes for
the e-mail to arrive, but generally it should be in your
Inbox or mailbox instantaneously. There are several ways
to retrieve mail, depending on which online service you use.

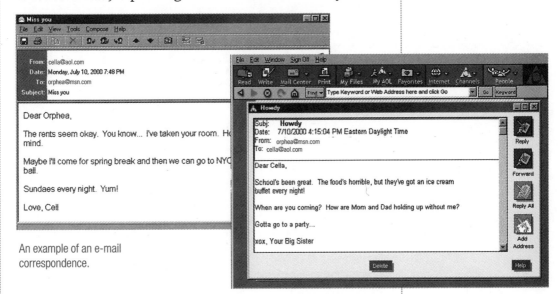

An example of an e-mail
correspondence.

Move the mouse arrow up to the word or icon for **Mail**
and click. Move the mouse arrow down to either **Read
Mail, Get New Mail** or **Get Messages** and click. Your
inbox or mailbox should appear on the screen.

Your new unread mail may either be in bold or have
some other indication that it hasn't been read. Double-click
on the mail to open it or, in some cases, click on the mail to
highlight it, then click on **Read**.

Another Item for
the Scrapbook

Let's print your new e-mail!
Is the printer plugged in and turned on?

Either click on the **Printer** icon in the Tool Bar or move the mouse arrow to the word **File**, click and then move the mouse arrow down to the word **Print** and click. When the Print window appears, hit **Enter**, **Return** or click on **Print**. Mission accomplished!

Reply to Sender . . . Address Is Known

You cannot send an anonymous e-mail. The sender's address will always appear on the e-mail. As a matter of fact, with some services the whole routing path will appear. (That is the indecipherable code at the top or bottom of your e-mail.)

To reply to the Sender (in this case, yourself), click once on **Reply, Reply to Sender** or **Reply to Author** that appears on the e-mail that you received. Each service is a little different, but you'll find the reply button easily.

Look what happened when you hit the **Reply** button! How convenient—an e-mail is all set up with the sender's (soon to be recipient's) e-mail address in the **To:** box. Now you can take it from here. Perhaps you want to try sending another e-mail to yourself. Better yet, do you have someone else's e-mail address? If no one you know has an e-mail address, it would be my pleasure to receive an e-mail from you. My e-mail address is: abby@abbyandme.com. It might take me a while, but I promise you'll get a response.

Forward March

An e-mail you receive can be passed on to others. To do this, click on the button that is labeled **Forward** or **Forward Message** in the open e-mail that you received.

> 66 *I love that I can e-mail at any time. I am often awake in the middle of the night and I would never think to call my girls at that time. When it happens now, I just sit at the computer and write them an e-mail.*99
>
> —Ed

The e-mail you got is now ready for you to forward. Click on the **To:** box and type in the e-mail address of the person you want to send it to. You can also type a message in the large text box if you want. Click on the text box and type away. When you're ready, simply click on the **Send** button to send both messages as one e-mail.

Your Little Black Book

Every online service has an address book where you can store the e-mail addresses of people that you will correspond with frequently. Click on the icon or the word **Mail**. Now click on **Address Book**. The address book will appear on the screen. Be extremely accurate when entering e-mail addresses. The last thing you want to have is a wrong address in your book.

Once you've put an e-mail address in the book, try sending an e-mail (you can start with mine if you don't have any others). You can either generate a new e-mail form when you have your address book open or you can open a new e-mail form and then access the address book from there. In either case, you must click on the address in the book and then click on either **To:** or **Send Mail**. Some services then ask you to click on **OK** to confirm your choice.

The real advantage of the address book is that you don't need to remember or keep typing e-mail addresses. This is handy because even a short e-mail address can be confusing.

Deleting Old Mail

Again, there will be several ways to delete old mail, depending on which service you use. When e-mail is open or even just highlighted, there might be a button with an **X** on it (not to be mistaken for the Close Box) or the word **Delete**. Click on whatever your service offers as a way to throw away read mail. It is wise to delete mail you don't need to keep. Anything you throw away from the computer gives it more space. More space gives you more speed. More speed gives you more enjoyment.

E-mail Etiquette

For some, sending an e-mail is bound to a code of conduct right up there with the rules of how to behave at a wedding or which fork to use at dinner. Take what you want and leave the rest behind.

1. You should always respond to an e-mail, even if it's only to acknowledge that it was received. *Unless it is an unwanted solicitation—I delete these immediately.*

2. Be selective about what you forward. Forwarding silly jokes you receive can be a bother for the recipient (ask if he or she wants them). Chances are, this isn't the first time these jokes have gone 'round the circuit.

3. Before you forward anything, try to clean it up by deleting all the gobbledegook that you may find at the beginning and end of the e-mail. Sometimes the list of who has seen the e-mail is longer than the message.

4. Retaliation for a "chain" e-mail that threatens bad luck unless it is sent to ten other people gets returned to the sender ten times. (I'm all for that!)

5. DON'T SHOUT! When you type in all caps, it is the equivalent of shouting at someone.

6. If you cc: an e-mail (send a carbon copy to someone), you're revealing the e-mail addresses of all the recipients. There are people who prefer to keep their e-mail address under wraps. Ask before you release it into the world.

7. Some online services offer a "buddy list." This alerts you to when someone on your buddy list comes

online while you're signed on. I find this terribly invasive. Shades of *1984*. Ask your buddies if they mind being added to your list.

Junk Mail

Eventually your e-mail address will get on someone's mailing list. Sad to say, even the Internet has junk mail. I delete junk mail right away. You can always reply to the sender that you want to be taken off the mailing list.

Be Adventurous

Click on and read all the different parts of your e-mail system. At this point you know how to get yourself out of an area that doesn't appeal to you. (Hint: Close Box!)

I have complete faith in your ability to dig deep into what your online service, the Internet and e-mail have to offer you. You have all the tools at your disposal. Be brave and strike out on your own.

Mind Your Ps & Qs
An introduction to word processing

Sherri's life is now stored on her computer. She uses her word-processing software to correspond and to keep track of dinner parties, birthdays and travel plans. You may not have a need for the word-processing software on your computer as much as she does, but at some point it'll come in handy and you'll be glad to know how to use it.

Two manufacturers of word-processing software dominate the market—Microsoft Word and WordPerfect. Some computers will come with one of these programs preinstalled.

"Software suites" are integrated software programs that combine word processing, spreadsheets, a database, graphics and/or communication options. Leading the market are the same manufacturers with Microsoft Works and PerfectWorks. If you think that you won't be doing a great deal more than word processing, there's no need to spend the extra money for a software suite. Stick with basic word-processing software.

This chapter involves a lot of instruction and hands-on work. Whenever you want to take a break, feel free. Do come back, however, and complete this chapter. Some of the editing tips will come in handy when you're writing an e-mail.

Meeting Your Word-Processing Program

Word-processing application software is used to write letters, make lists and do whatever else a typewriter was used for in the past. We're going to open your word-processing program, create a document and then play around with the options available to you.

Look at your desktop. Is there an icon for Microsoft Word or WordPerfect? If so, double-click on the icon.

If not and you are using a PC, click on **Start** (bottom left), then up to **Programs**. A large menu opened for you. Move your mouse onto **Microsoft Word** and click.

If there was no icon on the desktop and you are using a Mac, double-click on the **Hard Drive** (top right), then double-click on the **Applications** folder, then double-click on the **Microsoft Word** folder. (Almost done.) Once you see the **Microsoft Word** icon double-click on that.

If you don't see an option for Microsoft Word or WordPerfect, it may be that you don't have any word-processing software on your computer. That means you will need to purchase the software and install it. Don't hesitate to ask someone to help with this.

Use the Tutorial

A tutorial or tour will be included with your word-processing software. It may appear when you first open the software program or you can access it by clicking on the word **Help**. The tutorial will help you find your way around the program. Take the time to read the introduction it contains.

Starting from Scratch

MENU BAR   TOOL BAR

Now we have a blank slate in front of us. Let's see what the Menu Bar and Tool Bar have to offer and then we'll work with an actual document.

A Microsoft Word window contains a Menu Bar and Tool Bar. These will be used to edit, format and print documents.

Move the mouse arrow onto the word **File** on the Menu Bar and click. (With a Mac you may have to hold down the mouse button.) Read the commands available in this box. You may not know what each of these many instructions refer to, but it's valuable to be familiar with what's available. Do the same for each word in the Menu Bar. Click on the word and read what is contained in the box below.

Now slowly move the mouse arrow over the icons in the Tool Bar. As the mouse rests on each icon, a small box may appear that describes the task associated with that icon. Almost every task in the Menu Bar can also be accomplished with an icon in the Tool Bar. This allows you to take an action through a text format (the Menu Bar) or through a graphic format (the Tool Bar). Go with whatever suits you. I switch between the Menu and Tool Bar randomly.

Nice to Meet You

Move the mouse arrow onto the □ **New** (document) icon and click. Or you can move the arrow up to the word **File**, click and move down to the word **New** and click. A fresh, clean page will now present itself. Type the word "Hi."

The next thing we're going to do is name the document. In the Title Bar the name of your software package appears, and next to it are the words **Document 1** or possibly **Document 2**. Keep your eye on the Title Bar. After we rename this document, the new name will appear there.

Move the mouse arrow up to the word **File**, click and move it down to the words **Save As** and click. A window will appear where you can rename the document. Type the word "Smile" and hit **Enter**, **Return** or click on the **Save** button.

The Title Bar has now changed to reflect the new name of the document. Nicely done.

It's always best to name the document right at the beginning. If you get distracted or exit the program quickly

Oops—I Made a Mistake

If you make a mistake, you can erase your typing (from right to left) by using the **BkSp** (Backspace) or **Delete** key. (Either can usually be found on the upper right section of your keyboard next to the + = key.) Depress it once for each letter that you want to erase. You'll see that it moves from right to left, deleting whatever precedes it on the screen. If you hold your finger down on the key, it will continue to move and delete to the left until you lift your finger up. You definitely have more control when you depress and release the key with each character than when you hold the key down.

and forget to name the document, you'll be stuck sifting through a bunch of Documents 1, 2, 3, etc. It's easier to sort through documents whose names give a clue as to what they contain rather than a generic name.

See You Soon

I want you now to close the document that you renamed "Smile." I'm having you do this so that you experience what it's like to open an existing document.

Close the document by using the Close Box (either ☐ or ☒). On some word-processing programs there are two sets of Close Boxes. You'll have to be careful where you place the mouse arrow. One (in the Menu Bar) is for the document; the other (in the Title Bar) is for the software program itself. Don't close the software, but do close the document. Alternatively, you can move the mouse to the word **File**, click and move down to the word **Close** and click. Poof! Your "Smile" document is stored.

Welcome Back

Move the mouse arrow onto the 📂 **Open** icon and click. Or move the arrow to the word **File**, click and move it down to the word **Open** and click. Now you need to double-click on the document titled "Smile." If the double-clicking still proves troublesome, you can single-click on "Smile" and then hit the **Enter** or **Return** key or click **Open**. Your "Smile" document should appear.

Another way to open your document with some programs is to move the mouse arrow to the word **File**, click and move down to the bottom of the file box. The most recent documents that you've worked on may be listed here. Click once on "Smile" and it will open on the screen. If you want to try this technique, you can close the "Smile" document and reopen it this way.

Let's Get Typing

Open your "Smile" document if it isn't already on the screen. You will see a flashing vertical line in the left corner of the window. This is called the cursor. It indicates where typing will begin.

Please type the following:

My summer vacation

Make sure that the M is in uppercase. To do this, use the **Shift** key.

Notice that when the mouse arrow is in the text box, it changes to an I-beam instead of the arrow; this makes it easier to position between characters. Now insert the word "hot" before the word "summer" by moving the mouse

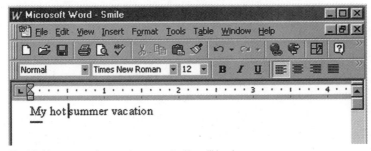

The blinking cursor shows where your typing will begin.

I-beam just before the "s" of "summer" and clicking once. The cursor is now before the "s" of "summer." Another way to change the location of the cursor is to use the arrow keys beside the right **Shift** key.

Once the cursor is properly positioned, type the word "hot." Did you notice that "summer" wasn't typed over but instead moved to the right to accommodate the new letters? (If this is not the case, depress and release the **Insert** key located on the bottom right of the keyboard.)

Now your screen should read:

My hot summer vacation

●   ## Save Me!

As I mentioned earlier in the book, it's very important that you regularly save the document you're working on. If the computer shuts off unexpectedly, the Smile document would exist, but the new text that we just typed would be lost.

Move the mouse arrow onto the word **File**, click and move the arrow down to the word **Save** and click. Such an important task and such an easy thing to execute.

Now we're going to move on to some editing tools. This is where the computer proves much more efficient than a typewriter. If you made a mistake with a typewriter or changed your mind about how you wanted your document to look, you would have no choice but to retype it. Not with a computer; it allows you to edit within the document before you print it out.

What if you decided that you wanted to move the first paragraph of a letter to the end of the letter? This would be accomplished by "cutting" the text from where it is and "pasting" it to a different location. Follow along and you'll see what I mean.

Move the cursor to the left of the word "hot." Do this with the mouse (remember to click) or with the arrow keys. Before the text can be altered, you must inform the computer of what text you want to change. This is accomplished by highlighting the text.

You can highlight the word "hot" several different ways:

Option 1. Click and drag the mouse arrow over the word "hot" and release the mouse button. (This is tricky at first, but it becomes easier with time.)

Option 2. Set the cursor at the start of the word "hot," depress the **Shift** key (on the left side of your keyboard) and hold it down. While the **Shift** is held down, use the arrow keys (on the right side of the keyboard) to move across the word.

Option 3. Move the mouse to the center of the word and double-click.

If You Goof

If you goofed when you tried to highlight, fear not. Simply move the mouse to a blank spot in the text box and click once—that will undo any highlighting. Go back and try again.

Using one of these methods, the word should now be highlighted. Of the three options, number 2 is the easiest to execute, but try them all and see which you prefer.

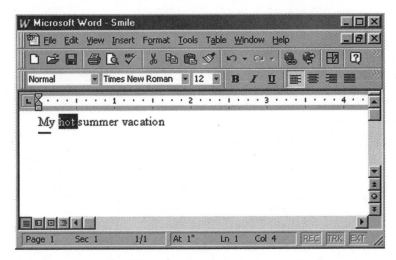

The word "hot" is now highlighted. This means the computer is waiting for your instructions for what to do with the word "hot".

You Must Cut Before You Paste

Now that you have highlighted the word "hot," you are able to either cut and paste text or copy and paste text.

Move the mouse arrow to the word **Edit** in the Menu Bar, click and then move it down to the word **Cut** and click. Right now the word "hot" has disappeared because the computer is storing the word until you tell it where to paste it. Now comes the paste!

• Move the cursor one space after the "n" of "vacation" by clicking the mouse after the "n" and then using the space bar.

• Move the mouse arrow to the word **Edit** and click.

• Then move it down to the word **Paste** and click. The word "hot" will now reappear after the word "vacation."

Instead of using the Menu Bar, you could have accomplished all of that with the icons in the Tool Bar.

✂ is the icon for **Cut** and 📋 is the icon for **Paste**. Try cutting and pasting again using the icons instead.

Copy That

Instead of cutting the text and pasting it, you might want to repeat a section of your document in another location. This is accomplished by copying and pasting the selected text.

Let's try to copy and paste.

• Go back to highlighting Options 1 through 3, pick one of the techniques and highlight the entire sentence. If you choose number 3 it takes a little practice, but place the cursor in the middle of the sentence and click the mouse three times in rapid succession. Double-click highlights a word—triple-click highlights the whole line.

• Move the mouse arrow to the word **Edit** in the Menu Bar, click and then move it down to the word **Copy** and click.

The sentence is still on the screen, but the computer has a copy of it stored until you tell it where you want it pasted.

• Place the cursor at the end of the sentence and hit **Enter** or **Return**.

• Move the mouse to the word **Edit** and click.

• Then move down to the word **Paste** and click.

• Repeat the two above actions five times. You should have a total of seven sentences on your screen. We'll use them next to show how many ways you can change the look of your text.

When you copy and paste, the original text stays in place and a copy of it appears wherever you choose to paste it. You can paste that copy as many times as you like.

Copying and pasting can also be done with the icons in the Tool Bar. 📋 represents **Copy**. 📋 represents **Paste**. Give it a try.

Complete Sentences

We're going to make this into a complete sentence.

Place the cursor just to the left of the "h" of "hot" in the first sentence, click to activate, and type the word "was." Your screen should now read:

My summer vacation was hot

Put a period at the end of the sentence by placing the cursor after the last word and hitting the period key.

Choices, Choices, Choices

There are so many different things that can be done to change the look of the text. All are done by highlighting text, which is a fundamental element with word processing. I'll run through a series of editing choices. Try each one now, then come back later and repeat the process until it starts to jell.

• Using whichever option you prefer (page 200) highlight the word "My" in the first sentence. Move the mouse arrow up to the **B** **Bold** icon in the Menu Bar and click once. The word **My** is now bold.

• Highlight the word "vacation" in the same sentence, move the mouse arrow to the *I* **Italics** icon in the Menu Bar and click once. The word *vacation* is now in italics.

• Highlight the word "hot" in the same sentence and move the mouse arrow to the **U** **Underline** icon in the Menu Bar. The word <u>hot</u> is now underlined.

You can change each word back to its original state by highlighting it, then reclicking on the icon that you used to make the change.

• Using whichever method you prefer (page 201), highlight the entire second sentence. Click on the ☰ **Center** icon in the Menu Bar.

The sentence is now in the center of the page.

Help

If you're ever stumped about how to do something and need help, simply move the mouse arrow onto the word **Help** in the Menu Bar and click. From there you can get all kinds of information. There may also be the option of clicking on a "?" question mark, then clicking where you need help and the screen will show some helpful hints pertaining to what you are doing.

• Highlight the entire third sentence. Click on the ☰ **Align Right** icon in the Menu Bar.

The sentence is now flush right on the page.

• Highlight the entire fourth sentence. Click on the ☰ **Align Left** icon in the Menu Bar.

The sentence is now flush left on the page.

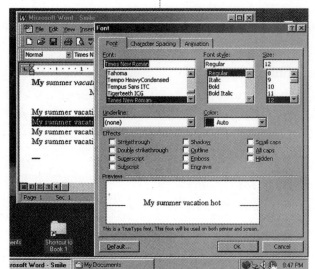

After you highlight text, the font can be changed by clicking on "Format," then "Font."

• Highlight the entire fifth sentence. Click on the word **Format** in the Tool Bar, then click on the word **Font.** This will reveal the different fonts (typefaces) available to you. Use the Scroll Bar to view the fonts. Click on whichever font appeals to you. The sentence could look like this **My vacation was hot,** or this *My vacation was hot,* or countless other ways, depending on which font you choose to use.

• Highlight the entire sixth sentence. Click on the arrow ▼ to the right of the font size box in the Menu Bar. Click on whichever size you want to see. This sentence could be My vacation was hot, or My vacation was hot.

Play with the different styles and

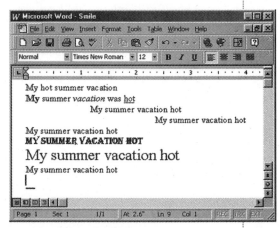

Play around with your document to try out all of the many editing and formatting possibilities.

sizes of fonts. But if you've been at the computer for a long time, sit back, take a breath and look around the room. When you've been focusing on the computer screen for a while, it's a good idea to give your eyes a break.

Repeat the exercises in this chapter as often as you can. It's only through repetition that you become comfortable with your word-processing software.

Smarter than the Average Bear

Your word-processing software is designed to make life easier. It even checks your spelling! Highlight the word "vacation" and retype it, spelling it "vaction." Note that when a word is highlighted and you start typing, the highlighted word disappears and the new word replaces it.

With some word-processing programs, a potentially misspelled word will have a red squiggly line under it. This is a heads-up that the word doesn't appear in the software's vocabulary list. You may also notice that some text may be underlined in green. This lets you know that the computer is questioning your grammar. Cheeky!

Let's perform a spell check on your document.

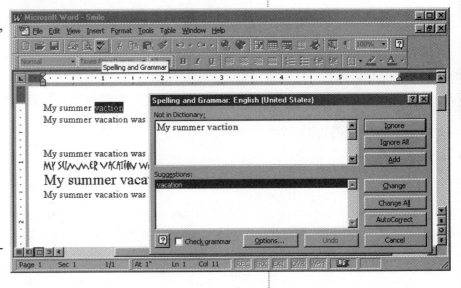

Microsoft Word (and most other word-processing programs) lets you spell check a document. Miraculous!

• Move the mouse arrow onto the ✓ **Spell Check** icon in the Menu Bar and click. The spell check will review the document for errors. In this case it will pick up that "vaction" is not in the dictionary and it will suggest "vacation."

• Click on the word **Change** or **Replace** in the Menu Bar. The computer will make the change and then either continue the spell check or let you know the spell check is complete.

The computer's dictionary may not contain a word that you have typed (such as a person's name or a technical term) and will signal that it appears to be wrong and should be corrected. However, if you know it's correct and should not be changed, you would click on **Ignore** or **Skip**.

A Souvenir

The last thing we'll do in this chapter is to print your first document. Make sure your printer is on.

Move the mouse arrow to the word **File** in the Menu Bar, click and move it down to the word **Print** and click.

There are several print options available in the **Print** window. You can print the current page that you're working on, all the pages of the document or select individual or groups of pages. You can also print as many copies of the document as you want. If you want to have one copy of all the pages and the print window is open,

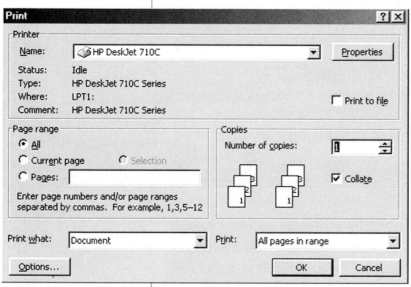

The Print window allows you to choose which pages to print and the number of copies you want.

simply hit the **Enter** or **Return** key or click on **Print**. The 🖨 **Print** icon won't offer all the choices that the **Print** window does, but it is a fast way to print the entire document.

You Deserve a Break Today

It's time to close the document. Move the mouse arrow to the word **File**, click and move down to the word **Exit** or **Quit** and click. You will now be asked if you want to save the changes made to the document. Click on either **Yes** or **Save**.

These are just the basic tools that your word-processing program offers. As you work more in the program, you will get better acquainted with what else it is capable of. If you ever get stuck, don't hesitate to call the software manufacturer's number for technical support.

What Can I Say?

It has been a pleasure joining you on this exciting adventure. Your homework is to go back over the last three chapters and repeat each of the exercises until they become second nature. Try to get on the computer every day for at least half an hour to keep from getting rusty. There's also a lot of very helpful information in the back of this book. Be sure to give it the once-over so you know what resources are available to you. Visit my web site **www.abbyandme.com** for additional guidance or just to say "Hi." Enjoy!

16 Troubleshooting—
I Think It Has a Fever
What to do if something doesn't seem right

Error messages that appear on a computer screen can cause the bravest souls to quake in their boots. These messages are generally as harmless as a spooky movie but can be just as frightening.

It's a good idea to keep a diary of any problems you have with your computer. Make a note of the date, time and what happened. If an error message appears on the screen, write it down exactly as it appears. This will prove a good resource for tracking errors. If indeed you bought a lemon, this will also be helpful information when you return the computer.

This chapter will go over some of the problems that you might come across with your computer. I want you to be aware of them and show you that they can be solved. Be assured that most of these problems will not happen. There is even the possibility that none of them will ever happen (although the chances of that are about the same as you winning the Publisher's Clearinghouse Sweepstakes). I don't expect you to understand the logic behind the solution; just read along to get a feel for how to troubleshoot problems. Consider this chapter your first-aid kit for your computer experience.

Take Advantage of Technical Support Services!

Technical support is yours for the taking, based on your warranty agreement. There is no question too big or too small to be asked. Read through the scenarios in this chapter, but know that you can always call for technical assistance instead of trying to troubleshoot on your own. You paid for the service—take advantage of it!

Bootstraps

Are you familiar with the saying "to pull someone up by their bootstraps"? That's what inspired the term "to boot" the computer. When you "boot" the computer, you're either straightening out a problem, restarting the computer or shutting it down.

Soft Boot = to close a program or restart the computer without shutting it down completely

Hard Boot = to shut down the computer by either turning it off or cutting off the electrical supply

Boot up = to turn on the computer

When I turned on the computer, the screen remained black.

Most monitors have a small light that indicates if the monitor is on. If this light is not lit, it means the monitor is not getting electricity.

1. Is the monitor turned on?
2. Is the computer plugged in?
3. Is the monitor plugged into the computer?
4. Is the computer plugged into a working outlet?
5. If it's plugged into a surge protector, is the surge protector plugged in and turned on?
6. There is a dial to increase or decrease the brightness of the screen somewhere on the monitor. Perhaps that is turned to the darkest choice. Find that dial and see if you can adjust the screen.

These solutions may seem too obvious to solve the problem, but that is often the case with computers. Because computers seem so complex, the simple solutions are sometimes overlooked. If only I had a dollar for every time a client called in distress and the culprit was a part of the computer that had been unplugged by accident.

My keyboard or mouse doesn't work.

Again, chances are something isn't plugged in correctly. Trace the path of each cord. Unplug the cord from its port and then replug it into the port. Sometimes even I find myself wondering why a document won't print, and then I remember I unplugged the printer the last time I took my laptop on the road. Oops. If it's still not working, try restarting your computer.

My mouse, keyboard or screen is frozen.

This remains one of the great mysteries of the computer. Sometimes it just freezes up on you. It's a bit like when a part of my brain can't come up with the name of a person I've known for years. Something stops working momentarily. The computer might fix itself in a few minutes, but if it doesn't, you can bring it back to life.

1. Rather than continue to click the mouse or hit the **Enter** key (on a PC) or the **Return** key (on a Mac), just get up from your desk and walk away. Some people get very frustrated when the computer freezes up. Be warned— computers cannot withstand the Samsonite stress test. Do *not* pound on your keyboard or your mouse. It will only make matters worse. If you need to take five, do so. By the time you come back to the computer, it may have adjusted itself.

2. You can try gently depressing the **Esc** (Escape) key a couple of times (the Esc key is usually at the top left of the keyboard). The Esc key is used to get out of a program or to stop an action before it is completed.

3. If the Esc key doesn't help, you will need to "soft boot" (or "force quit" in Mac speak) the computer. To soft boot means to close a program that isn't responding or, if that doesn't work, to force the computer to restart or shut down without pulling the plug. To "hard boot" the computer is a last resort and involves cutting off the electricity (by shutting off the computer or unplugging it) rather than following the proper shutdown process. My interpretation is that you're giving the computer a swift kick with a soft boot as opposed to a hard boot. We won't hard boot the computer unless absolutely necessary. Of course, you should never really kick the computer, with or without footwear!

To soft boot a PC:

- Find the **Ctrl** (Control), **Alt** (Alternate) and **Del** (Delete) keys on your keyboard.
- Hold all three down simultaneously, then release.
- A **Close Program** window will appear. It will list all the programs that are open.

No Need to Rush

When an error message appears on your screen or your machine does something you don't understand, there's usually no need to rush to fix it. Write down the error message, if one has appeared, then just leave the computer on (error message and all) until you get help. You won't do it any harm.

• Hit the **Enter** key. That instructs the computer to **End Task**. That means the computer will close the program that is highlighted in blue. (This program may have the words "not responding" next to it.) You'll then be asked to confirm this choice. Hit the **Enter** key again to confirm.

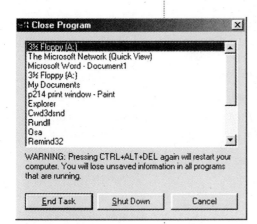

When a PC freezes, first try the Close Program window to close a program that is not responding.

• If that doesn't work, hold down the **Ctrl, Alt** and **Del** keys again and release.

• The **Close Program** window will reappear. If you can move the mouse arrow to the words **Shut Down,** do so and click once. If your mouse is also frozen, then hold down the **Ctrl, Alt** and **Del** keys one more time and release again.

• This will instruct the computer to restart. It's a more gentle solution than hard booting the computer, which involves turning the computer off by cutting off the electrical current.

The computer may have frozen because the program you were in had a hiccup of sorts, not because the computer has any real problems. That's why we first look at the programs that are open and see if closing one of them will unfreeze the computer.

To soft boot a Mac:

• Find the ⌘ (Command), **Option Alt** and **Esc** (Escape) keys on your keyboard.

• Hold all three down simultaneously, then release.

• The "**Force** [whatever program you are in] **to quit?**" question will appear.

• Hit the **Return** key. That instructs the computer to **Force Quit**. That means the computer will close the program that is probably causing the problem.

• If that doesn't work, hold down the ⌘ (Command), **Option Alt** and **Esc** keys at the same time and then release.

• This will instruct the computer to restart. It's a more

gentle solution than hard booting the computer, which involves cutting the electrical current by turning the computer off.

4. If a soft boot fails, you have no choice but to hard boot (shut down) the computer. You do this by turning the power switch off on the computer. If that doesn't work, you'll have to unplug the computer or turn off the surge protector. Count to 20 and then turn the computer back on. Everything should be fine now.

Force "Microsoft Word" to quit?
Checking Force Quit causes you to lose any unsaved changes. To avoid further problems, restart your computer after you click Force Quit.

(Force Quit) (Cancel)

When a Mac freezes, the Force Quit window will help you to "soft boot" the machine.

Note: When you close a program through a soft or hard boot, you can't save any of the changes that you've made. *Translation: You were writing a letter to your son and the computer froze. You soft or hard booted the computer to unfreeze it. The parts of the letter that you had not saved will not be there when you retrieve it.*

● My PC screen has a strange disk error message.

A:>
Non-System disk or disk error.
Replace and strike any key when ready

Don't worry! You only forgot to take your floppy disk out of the A: drive. Remove the disk and press any key (whatever key that your little heart desires) on the keyboard. Your computer should continue the startup process without a glitch.

A "Microsoft Windows (95 or 98) Startup Menu" appeared on my PC screen.

```
Microsoft Windows (95 or 98)
Startup Menu
===========================
1.  Normal
2.  Logged (/BOOTLOG.TXT)
3.  Safe Mode
4.  Step-by-step conformation
5.  Command Prompt Only
6.  Safe mode command prompt only
Enter a choice: 1
```

This window will appear on a PC if something went wrong during the startup process. For right now, we don't care what went wrong. We just want to get the computer back on track. In this case the first thing to do is to hard boot (turn off) the computer, count to 20 and turn it back on.

If the box appears again, choose option 3 by typing the number 3 and hitting the **Enter** key. Your computer will go into "safe mode." From there we will shut it down by moving the mouse arrow to the **Start** button (on the bottom left of your screen) and clicking the mouse once. Then move the arrow up to the words **Shut Down** and click once. A **Shutdown Window** will appear in the center of your screen; move the mouse arrow to the word **Restart** and click once.

Next, hit the **Enter** key. This will allow your computer to restart and all should be cured.

I'm sure all of this sounds a bit unappealing, but it really isn't that bad when you're doing it. Trust me.

My PC screen is black except for this: C:\DOS>.

On a PC this is called the DOS prompt. Try typing in the

word "win" and hitting the **Enter** key. This may bring the desktop screen up. If that doesn't work, then turn off the computer (hard boot), count to 20 and turn it back on.

The Sad Mac

For Mac users, you're greeted every time you start up the computer with an image of a sweet, smiling Mac. Well, he has an evil twin that you don't want to meet. If the frowning Mac should appear on your screen, you need technical assistance. You can ask a friend who has a Mac to help, but you might need someone with more technical knowledge. Whatever has gone wrong can be fixed. Now is the time to take advantage of the terms of your warranty.

My screen says an error has occurred.

```
A Type 1 error has occurred.
```
Gulp!

This Mac error message leads one to believe that identifying it as a type 1 or 2 or 10,000 error would help solve the problem, but that isn't the case. For us civilians we can only glean from that message that we should restart the computer.

- Hold down the ⌘ **Command, Option/Alt** and **ESC** keys at the same time and then release.
  - This will instruct the computer to restart.

This error message shouldn't happen often, if at all. Keep a record of when it occurs. If it happens frequently, it would be wise to have the machine serviced.

The computer won't let me delete a file or document.

Chances are the document or folder you want to delete is still open. Make sure that you've closed the document or folder and quit the program that it lives in.

Better Safe than Sorry

As I mentioned in Chapter 5, computers have several enemies.

• A magnet held over a floppy disk can delete everything stored on that disk. Magnets can also damage the screen and other components in your computer case. My advice— keep your magnets on the fridge and nowhere near your computer.

• Liquids should be kept *far away* from your keyboard. As you may recall, it was just a few drops of milk from my cereal spoon that caused a huge amount of damage. Don't take that chance. Instead, take regular breaks from the computer and enjoy your refreshing drink away from the machine. Any excuse to get up from the computer helps prevent bleary eyes and fatigue anyway.

• Little kids are the wunderkinder of computers. However, they may not be gentle with your keyboard or mouse. Never let children use your computer unsupervised.

• Static electricity is another villain. I recently read an article that a woman's computer at work conked out every day at 4:45 P.M. Several technicians tried to find the problem, but to no avail. Finally, a technician decided to observe her at that hour. What he discovered was that as her workday came to a close she would get more and more anxious about finishing her work on time. She would cross and recross her legs, conducting static electricity from the thick carpet below her desk, which in turn fouled up her computer. It isn't wise to have the computer in a room with a heavy pile carpet.

• Be sure to protect your floppy diskettes and CD-ROMs from any extremes. They don't respond well to direct sunlight or heat. The safest thing to do is to store them in a box or on a bookshelf. I used to keep mine on a shady windowsill until my cleaning woman accidentally sent them on a four-story Kamikaze drop. Splat. Now I have them safely stored under my desk.

Achoo! Is It a Cold or a Virus?

It's true, a computer can have a virus, and that virus can reproduce itself inside the computer or move from one computer to another via an e-mail attachment or a floppy disk.

A virus can manifest itself in a variety of ways. You may notice that your computer functions more slowly than usual or that certain tasks aren't being carried out properly. Unfortunately, a virus can also destroy information stored on your computer.

The nasty truth about viruses is that they are manmade. They are the result of some computer geek's wanting to see how insidious his virus can become. Viruses can be debilitating, but they can also be detected and destroyed with virus software. Your computer probably came with virus detection software. If not, ask your salesperson about it.

Boo!

I just threw a lot of "ifs" and bad scenarios at you. This is all meant to empower you: knowing that you have the resources available should something go wrong with your computer.

I would love to tell you that your computer will never have a problem, but I would be lying to you. Computers were made by humans and they have flaws. I hope that, between this book and the instructional book that came with your machine, a solution is never too far away.

Updating Your Virus Detection Software

Because new viruses are being created everyday, you will need to update your computer to protect it from the newest incarnation. The virus software that you buy will offer this feature. Be sure to take advantage of it by either sending in your registration card or accessing their web site.

Some Recommended Web Sites

(**Reminder:** You don't need to precede a web site address with **http//:**, but you may need to precede the address with **www**.)

Antiques
antiques-oronoco.com/
antiquesroadshow.com
ehammer.com
icollector.com

Car Buying
autobytel.com
autoweb.com
invoicedealers.com
nada.com

Classifieds
buylines.com
loot.com
wantadpress.com
yankeetrader.com

Community
geocities.com
ivillage.com
tripod.com

Company Info.
companiesonline.com
companysleuth.com
hoovers.com
intellifact.com
kompass.com

Computer Gizmos
cnet.com
computers.com
curtisconnections.com
keyspan.com

Family
babycenter.com
family.com
parents.com

Film
hit-n-run.com
imdb.com
reel.com

Find Someone
bigbook.com
infospace.com
infousa.com
peoplesearch.net
peopleyahoo.com
switchboard.com
teldir.com
whowhere.com

Food
epicurious.com
foodtv.com
globalgourmet.com
kitchenlink.com
tavolo.com
vegweb.com

Fun(ny)
jokeaday.com
loftcam.com/trick.html
theonion.com

Good Deeds
care2.com
give.org
hungersite.com
rainforest.care2.com

Greeting Cards (Free)
123greetings.com
bluemountain.com
egreetings.com
postcards.com

Grocery Shopping
netgrocer.com
peapod.com
shoprite.com
stopandshop.com
shaws.com
stew-leonards.com

History
thedropzone.org

Household
replacements.com
setyourtable.com
toiletology.com

Investing
bloomberg.com
cnbc.com
fool.com
ka-ching.com
marketguide.com
thestreet.com
wsj.com

Jobs
bls.gov
careermosaic.com
careerpath.com
dbm.com/jobguide
employmentspot.com
espan.com
jobtrak.com
monster.com

Magazines
drudge.com
salon.com
slate.com
smithsonianmag.si.edu

Medical
ama-assn.org
drweil.com
healthfinder.gov
healthy.net/selfcare
intelihealth.com
mayohealth.org
medscape.com
nejm.com
quackwatch.com
webmd.com

Miscellaneous
bbbonline.org
 (Better Business
 Bureau)
abuse.net
 (to report Internet
 bad behavior)

Music
mp3.com
music.com
sonicnet.com

News
cnn.com
msnbc.com
nytimes.com

Politics
freedomforum.org
e-thepeople.com

Research
infoplease.com
pbs.org
refdesk.com

Science
exploratorium.edu
nationalgeographic.com
sciam.com

Search Engines
askjeeves.com
askme.com
directhit.com
dogpile.com
google.com
yahoo.com

Seniors
aarp.org
agenet.com
elderhostel.org
eldertreks.com
grandmabetty.com
grouptravelleader.com
nsclc.org
senior.com
seniornet.org
seniorssearch.com
ssa.gov
thirdage.com

Shopping
amazon.com
bluefly.com
dealtime.com
deja.com
ebay.com
epinions.com
etoys.com
macys.com
mysimon.com
presentpicker.com
rusure.com

Sports
espn.com
sportingnews.com
sportspages.com
stats.com

Travel
biztravel.com
cheaptickets.com
citysearch.com
cnn.com
expedia.com
frommers.com
mapquest.com
previewtravel.com
roadsideamerica.com
roughguides.com
skiersover50.com
skyauction.com
timeout.com
travelocity.com
travelscape.com
tripspot.com

Glossary

A: drive the part of the computer where you insert a floppy disk (*see* disk drive)

Apple a personal computer (also referred to as a MAC or Macintosh) with a unique operating system

application software software that allows you to perform specialized tasks, such as word processing

arrow keys keys on the keyboard that allow you to move the cursor around the screen

bits per second (bps) measurement of a modem's data transmission speed

bookmark a web site address saved to be revisited (also referred to as "favorite")

boot up to turn on the computer

browser a software program (such as Netscape Navigator or Microsoft Internet Explorer) that allows your computer to communicate with the World Wide Web

byte a measurement of space; a byte equals a single alphabetic or numeric character

caps lock key a key on the keyboard that allows you to type in upper case until it is deactivated by depressing and releasing the key again

CD-ROM a disk that holds software to be installed onto the computer; FYI: CD-ROM stands for "compact disc, read-only memory" (thankfully you will never need to remember that)

central processing unit (CPU) the part of the computer that serves as the pathway for all information

chat room place on the Internet where people communicate live by sending typed messages back and forth

click depressing and releasing the mouse button to take an action

click and drag an action taken with the mouse to move items on the screen, such as a solitaire card or an icon

clone an old term that refers to non-IBM PCs

close box the box in your title bar where you click to close a window

collapse box the box in a Mac title bar where you click to shrink a window

computer case the part of the computer that houses the CPU, hard drive, RAM, modem and disk drives

copy an editing tool that allows you to copy text and use it elsewhere in a document

crashing an overly dramatic reference to the computer unintentionally shutting off

cut an editing tool that allows you to remove text from one area of a document and insert it in another area

cyberspace a figurative reference to the intangible world of the Internet, such as the World Wide Web and e-mail, visited by a computer user

D: drive (or E: drive) a part of the computer where you insert a CD-ROM either to read or listen to its contents (*see* disk drive)

desktop (1) a non-laptop computer (2) the name for the main screen display on the computer (whether it is a laptop or a desktop)

disk drive a part of the computer that reads information or software from a disk

domain name a person's or organization's chosen web site name, including the suffix that identifies the type of web site (for example: www.whitehouse.gov)

double-click quickly depressing and releasing the mouse button twice on an icon or text to take an action, such as to open a document or a software program

drag *see* click and drag

e-mail (electronic mail) to send or receive typed messages via the Internet

e-mail address a person's or organization's chosen address where they would receive e-mail (e.g., abby@abbyandme.com)

emoticon a playful use of keyboard characters and symbols to represent emotional responses (also referred to as smileys), usually used in e-mail or in chat rooms, i.e., >: -(means angry

Enter or Return key a keyboard feature that performs actions; also can be used like a return key on a typewriter when typing a document or e-mail

error message a message from the software indicating that an error has occurred; sometimes a code or number is given in the message so a technician can identify the problem

external modem a modem outside the computer, connected by a cable

favorite *see* bookmark

floppy disk a disk that either holds information to be installed on the computer or is used to copy information from your computer

font a style of type

freezing a reference to when the mouse and keyboard become temporarily inoperative

function keys a set of keys on the keyboard, rarely used nowadays, that carry out special commands

gigabyte (GB) a measurement of computer hard-drive space; roughly 1,000 megabytes

hacker a highly skilled computer user who gains entry to information on computers not intended for them by "cracking" the programming codes

hard boot to shut down the computer when it is frozen, either by switching it off or by cutting off the electrical supply

hard drive (C: drive) a place in the computer where information is permanently stored

hardware the physical pieces of a computer (i.e., monitor, mouse, keyboard, computer case)

hertz a measurement of computer processor speed

Home Page the first page of any web site on the Internet

http (hypertext transfer protocol) a prefix to a web site address (which no longer needs to be typed in) that helps direct your browser software to the web site

i-beam one of the many faces of the mouse; designed to fit between the characters of text to make changes

IBM compatible any PC that works with software designed for the IBM (*see* clone)

icon a small picture or image that represents a software program, a document or a command

information superhighway a reference to the seemingly limitless information of the World Wide Web

installing process where software is read and stored on the hard drive

internal modem a modem that is housed inside the computer case

Internet a huge worldwide, ever-growing system of computers linked by data or phone lines

Internet service provider (ISP) a company that provides access to the Internet

keyboard used to type information into the computer

laptop a portable non-desktop computer that combines the drivers, keyboard, mouse and monitor into one much smaller unit

link a web site feature that when clicked on will take you to more information on the subject indicated

login name a unique name chosen by a user to identify him or her while on the Internet

login password private set of letters or numbers used to confirm the identity of the computer user

log off disconnecting from the Internet (also referred to as signing off)

log on connecting to the Internet (also referred to as signing on)

Mac or Macintosh *see* Apple

maximize box the box on a PC title bar that allows you to increase the size of a window

megabyte (MB) a measurement of computer space

megahertz (MHz) a measurement of computer processor speed

menu bar the bar that appears below the title bar in a window and offers menus to different commands

minimize box the box on a PC title bar that allows you to shrink a window

modem the part of the computer that allows you to connect to the Internet through a phone line

monitor the part of the computer that houses the screen; measured diagonally from top corner to opposite bottom corner

mouse device to move the pointer on the screen

mouse buttons controls on the top of the mouse that you click to carry out a command (*see* click)

mouse pad a pad where you rest the mouse to control its movement

netiquette network etiquette; a protocol for how to communicate your ideas or feelings via e-mail or chat rooms (e.g., USE OF CAPS INDICATES THAT YOU ARE SHOUTING)

newbie a new person to the Internet

notebook computer *see* laptop

online service provider *see* Internet service provider

operating software the system (such as Windows 2000 or Mac OS8) that organizes and manages your computer

paste an editing tool that allows you to place text that you have cut or copied

PC (PC compatible) *see* IBM compatible

peripherals additional pieces of hardware, such as a printer or scanner, attached to the computer

personal computer any computer intended to be used by one person (includes IBM compatibles and Macs).

pirated software the illegal practice of copying software purchased by someone else

pointer an arrow that appears on the screen and moves according to the manipulation of the mouse; also referred to as the arrow, mouse arrow or cursor

port a part of the computer where the cables from the different computer parts are plugged in

printer allows you to print information from the computer

RAM (random access memory) temporary memory used when the computer is on

right click a function offered on the PC mouse that allows for more advanced tasks

scanner copies images and text into the computer

scroll bar a feature that allows you to move a page up and down to expose all its contents

scroll box a part of the scroll bar that allows you to control the movement of the page

search engine a web site where you can search for information on a given topic

shift key a key on the keyboard that performs several functions including typing in uppercase or highlighting text

snail mail a negative reference to the time it takes for the postal service to deliver mail in contrast to the speed with which an e-mail is sent

soft boot to close a program or restart the computer without completely shutting it down

start page the first page of an online service

surfing the net traveling the Internet from site to site

surge protector protects the computer from irregular electrical currents

task bar the bar that appears at the bottom of a PC screen that contains the start button as well as access to other programs and features

title bar the bar that appears at the top of a window and indicates the name of the software program and the document; also contains the close box

touch point type of mouse used on a laptop that uses a small rubber button for control (*see* mouse)

trackball type of mouse that uses a ball for control (*see* mouse)

Uniform Resource Locator (URL) a technical name for a web site address

upgrading hardware increasing the capacity of the computer

upgrading software installing a new and improved generation of a software program already installed on the computer

user name *see* login name

user password *see* login password

virus a problem on the computer created by malcontent computer geeks; viruses are meant to damage computers and are spread by opening e-mail attachments or using someone else's floppy disks

virus protection software helps detect and destroy viruses

web page any page that follows the Home Page of a web site

welcome page *see* start page

window a term describing the visual frame that appears on your computer screen

Windows 98, 2000 the operating system used on most PCs

World Wide Web (WWW) a cyberspace library of information organized by web site

wrist pad helps prevent wrist strain

"writeable" CD-ROM functions like a CD-ROM, but can also copy information from your computer

zoom box the box on a Mac title bar where you click to increase the size of a window

Resource List

Here are phone numbers you may find useful (unfortunately, these numbers are subject to change).

Computer Manufacturers and Technical Support

Acer America 800-637-7000
Alliance for Technology Access
  (for the disabled) 800-455-7970
Apple/Macintosh 800-538-9696
Compaq 800-652-6672
Dell 800-624-9896
Epson America 800-922-8911
Fujitsu 800-345-0845
Gateway 800-846-2301
Hewlett Packard 800-475-3331
IBM 800-237-5511
Keytronic (ergonomic keyboards)
  800-262-6006
Toshiba 800-457-7777

Printer Manufacturers and Technical Support

Brother International 800-276-7746
Canon 800-848-4123
Epson 800-922-8911
Hewlett Packard 800-752-0900
Panasonic 800-726-2797

User Groups

Association of PC User Groups
  914-876-6678
Mac User Group Connection
  800-538-9696

Online Services

America Online 800-227-6364
AT&T 800-967-5363
CompuServe 800-848-8199
Eathlink 800-395-8425
Microsoft Network 206-882-8080
Prodigy 800-776-3449

Software Manufacturers and Technical Support

Word-processing Suites

Microsoft 800-426-9400
Perfect Office Novell 800-453-1267
SmartSuite – Lotus 800-343-5414

Financial Management Software

Microsoft Money 800-426-9400
Peachtree 800-247-3224
Quicken – Intuit 800-446-8848

Virus Software

Dr. Solomon/McAfee 972-308-9960
Norton Anti-Virus – Symantec
  800-441-7234

Mail-Order Houses

PC Connection 800-800-0005
PC Zone 800-258-8088
MicroWarehouse 800-367-7080
MacWarehouse 800-255-6227
The Mac Zone 800-248-0800

Magazines

Computer User 800-365-7773
PC Magazine 800-289-0429
PC World 800-234-3498
Macworld 800-288-6848

Test-Drive Form

1. **Store:** _____
   Salesperson: _____
   Note the address and phone number of the store and the name of the salesperson you spoke with.

2. **Brand & Model of Computer:** _____
   Include any numbers that follow the brand name—this will indicate the model. For example: Toshiba Satellite 100CS.

3. **Cost:** _____
   Note the basic cost and any additional costs. For example: $1,499 plus $199 for 20MB RAM upgrade = $1,698.

SYSTEM INFORMATION

4. **Computer Case:** ☐ Standard   ☐ Tower
   Is the computer case a standard model or a tower model, which will go on the floor?

5. **CPU Speed:** _____   Upgradeable ☐ Yes   ☐ No
   Remember, the CPU speed is measured in megahertz (MHz). You will need a CPU with at least 300MHz, but if you want to splurge, you could go as high as 800MHz, or even higher.

6. **RAM:** _____ Upgradeable ☐ Yes   ☐ No
   The RAM size is measured in megabytes (MB). You will want a RAM size of at least 64MB—but 128MB is more fun.

7. **Hard Drive:** _____ Upgradeable ☐ Yes   ☐ No
   The hard drive size is also measured in megabytes or gigabytes (GB). I recommend that you start with 6GB. There is no need to exceed 10GB for almost anything you could think of doing on the computer.

8. **Monitor Size:** _____
   Monitor size is measured in diagonal inches from a top corner to the opposite bottom corner of the screen itself. For most, a bigger screen is better, but you can judge what suits you best by checking out several different sizes. A flat-panel screen takes up less space on your desk and has better resolution but is more expensive.

9. **Screen Type:**   Active ☐   Passive ☐

There are two types of screens if you are looking at a laptop with a 13" screen—active and passive. An active screen has a bit more clarity and can be viewed from all angles as clearly as it can straight on. A passive screen can be viewed clearly only from the front. An active screen is substantially more expensive. Make sure you view both types and decide if you think it is worth the extra money for the active screen.

10. **Modem Speed:** _____

Modem speed is measured in kilobytes (KB) per second. Don't linger on this: the higher, the better. If it is included with your computer, the modem will be an internal one. Older machines offer 28KB modems, but most of my students go for a 56KB modem and you should as well. If an internal modem is not included, go to point 38 to record the modems you've seen.

11. **Speakers Included:**   Yes ☐   No ☐
12. **Headphones:**   Yes ☐   No ☐
13. **Microphone:**   Yes ☐   No ☐
14. **Fax Capability:**   Yes ☐   No ☐

Numbers 11 through 14 are merely to note whether those features are included with the computer. The choice of machine is not necessarily made by the number of times you check "yes." It is based on which of the features matter to you.

15. **Type of Mouse:** _____   **Notes on Feel:** _____

If you are buying a desktop, it will come with a standard mouse. If you are buying a laptop, note which kind of mouse it comes with (trackball, touchpad, touchpoint). Jot down some notes on the feel of each. Remember, you can't be expected to master the mouse at this point, but you will have an impression of how it feels. Is the mouse positioned in a place that seems easy to access, or is your hand cramped while using it? Your mouse will be your constant companion when you're on the computer, so it must be comfortable to access and control. But generally speaking, control will come with practice.

16. **Notes on Keyboard:** _____

Note the feel of the keyboard. Do the keys feel mushy? Are they too resistant? Or are they just right?

17. **How Will It Fit in Your Workspace?** _____

Take notes on how you picture your computer system in your home.

SUPPORT

18. **Warranty:**_____

    The length of the warranty will be in months. What parts fall under warranty?

19. **Extended Warranty:**_____**Cost:**_____

    It's more than likely that the computer store where you make your purchase will offer you an extended warranty. This is an agreement with the store or mail-order company, not the manufacturer. The agreement is valid only if the store is still operational for the duration of the extended warranty—a good reason to make sure you are shopping at a reputable store.

20. **Money-Back Guarantee:**_____

    This may be an agreement with the manufacturer that you have a certain number of days to return the machine—kind of like the lemon law. Beware: some manufacturers will not exchange a computer even if it is defective. They may only offer to repair the machine. In that case you may want to engage your credit card company as an advocate for you. Or, before contacting the manufacturer, call the store you purchased it from and ask if it is willing to exchange the defective computer.

21. **Technical Support:**   Yes ☐   No ☐

    This is crucial. You want to make sure that the store or mail-order company you purchase from has technical support. The last thing you want to have to do is pack up your computer and mail it to the manufacturer. It is irritating enough to have to bring it to the store for repairs. Ask specifically about telephone technical support. A lot of questions or problems can be answered by a telephone call to a technician.

    You should be getting free support for the length of your warranty, whether you have a problem with your computer or you have a question about how to use the machine.

    If the manufacturer, not the store, provides the technical support, ask your salesperson for the technical repair number of the manufacturers you are considering. When you are home, call the number and see how long it takes for you to speak to a technician. I've been on hold with some for over 20 minutes. This could be a deciding factor in determining which computer you purchase.

22. **On-Site Repair:**   Yes ☐   No ☐   **Cost:**_____

    Can someone come to your home to repair your computer? How much will it cost if it is still under warranty? What if the warranty has expired?

23. **On-Site Installation:** Yes ☐   No ☐   **Cost:**_____

    Can someone come to your house to install your system?

SOFTWARE

24. Operating System:_____
   Preinstalled Software:_____
   Note the operating system in your computer (Windows 98, Windows 2000, Mac OS9, other) and any preinstalled application software.

25. Additional Software:_____**Cost:**_____
   Additional Software:_____**Cost:**_____
   You may want to buy word-processing software or some other software based on your interest. We will talk about this choice in Chapter 8.

PRINTER

26. Brand Name & Model:_____
   Include any numbers that follow the brand name—they will indicate the model.

27. Cost:_____

28. Features: Color ☐   Black & White Only ☐
                        Fax ☐   Copy ☐   Scanner ☐

   You will choose features based on your specific needs. A basic black-and-white printer may be all that you want. A color printer and scanner might be helpful if you decide to do something like a family newsletter or to make your own greeting cards. Color is also more fun if you're printing a web site. However, if you use a color printer, you have to purchase both a black ink cartridge and a color ink cartridge. Cartridges can be pricey.

29. Paper Loading: Top ☐   Front ☐
   It is important to note whether the printer is front or top loading so you can arrange your workspace accordingly.

30. Number of Pages Printed per Minute:_____
   If you are anticipating a lot of printing, how quickly the printer works may be quite important to you.

31. **Number of Pages Printed per Ink Cartridge:**_____

    This is an important issue. I have a student who was interested in having a small, portable printer. She was unpleasantly surprised when her ink cartridge ran out after less than 50 pages were printed and a replacement cartridge cost over $20.

32. **Cost of Ink Cartridge Replacements:**_____

33. **Length of Warranty:**_____

34. **Extended Warranty:**_____**Cost:**_____

    To repeat from point 19, it's more than likely that the computer store where you make your purchase will offer you an extended warranty. This is an agreement with the store, not the manufacturer. The agreement is valid only if the store is still operational for the duration of the extended warranty—a good reason to make sure you're shopping at a reputable store.

35. **Money-Back Guarantee:** _____

    Full refund ☐   Store credit ☐   Other ☐

    Again, this is an agreement with the manufacturer that you have a certain number of days to return the machine. Ask the store if you get a full refund or just a store credit.

36. **Toll-Free Support:**   Yes ☐   No ☐

    Remember, this is crucial. You want to make sure that the store you purchase from has technical support. You should be getting free support for the length of your warranty.

37. **On-Site Repair:**   Yes ☐   No ☐   **Cost:**_____

    Even with the printer, ask if someone can come to your home to repair it.

MODEM

(If a modem is not included with your computer, you will want to buy an external modem.)

38. **Brand Name & Model:**_____
    Include any numbers that follow the brand name—they will indicate the model.

39. **Speed:**_____
    The higher, the better. Go for nothing less than a 56K modem.

40. **Cost:**_____

41. **Warranty:**_____
    Length of warranty in months.

42. **Extended Warranty:**_____**Cost:**_____
    I am not sure this is really necessary for a modem, but let the salesperson explain why you might need it if the store is offering an extended warranty.

43. **Money-Back Guarantee:**_____
    Again, this is an agreement with the manufacturer that you have a certain number of days to return the modem.

44. **Toll-Free Support:**   Yes ☐   No ☐
    Remember, this is crucial. You want to make sure that the store you purchase from has technical support. You should be getting free support for the length of your warranty.

45. **Did you ask if all of the peripherals are compatible?**
    Make sure that all the parts you are buying are friendly with each other. Have your salesperson confirm this and note his or her name in case he or she is wrong.

Index

(Page numbers in *italic* refer to illustrations.)

ANNOUNCING
abbyandme.com

....

Take a web tutorial. Learn to send e-mail. Ask Abby your most pressing computer questions. Plus discover how to use search engines and follow some of the best links on the web. It's all at **www.abbyandme.com**, and here's how to get there:

1. Move your mouse arrow onto the icon on your desktop screen that connects you to the Internet and double-click. You may hear some noise when the modem connects—don't worry, that just means the modem is working.

2. Your online service may remember your user name and password. If it doesn't, type in your user name. Move into the password text box by either hitting the **Tab** key on your keyboard or move the mouse arrow into the text box and click to activate it. Type your password. Click on the button to **sign on**. (Be patient while your computer connects to the Internet—this may take a moment or two.)

3. Some Internet service providers will open right to a web browser (the program you'll use to surf the Internet), where you can enter the address. If this is true for you (you'll see a text box that says **Address**), skip to step 4. Other Internet service providers require another step—look for the Internet Explorer or Netscape icon on your desktop. Double-click on it and this will launch your browser. Now you can proceed to step 4.

4. Move your mouse arrow into the web site address box that appears near the top of the window and click once.

5. Type in www.abbyandme.com.

6. Hit the **Enter** or **Return** key on your keyboard or move the mouse arrow onto the word **Go** and click.

7. Congratulations! You made it! Take your time and enjoy yourself.